Classroom Blogging:

A Teacher's Guide
To Blogs, Wikis,
& Other Tools
that are Shaping
a New
Information
Landscape

2nd Edition

By David F. Warlick

David F. Warlick can be reached at

david@landmark-project.com

Support information for this book can be found at:

http://landmark-project.com/classblogging/readers/

Acknowledgments

Without the ideas, insights, and enthusiasm of a growing number of blogging educators, this book would not have happened. It would be impossible to mention all of the names. But three names cannot go unspoken. Steve Dembo introduced me to podcasting, and continues to be a source of support, ideas, and inspiration. Will Richardson introduced us all to blogging in the classroom through his presentation at the National Educational Computing Conference, and he continues to be a prime source of ideas about teachers in the blogosphere.[*] As with all of my books, I want to express another special thank you to Paul Gilster, for his continued support, suggestions, and our regular coffees – during which he teaches me about the emerging technologies that are beyond the understanding of anyone else I know. Buy his excellent book about the future of interstellar space travel, <u>Centauri Dreams</u> (ISBN 038700436X).

I must also thank, again, the first computer visionary I ever knew, my father, who taught me how to ask questions, and to my mother, who taught me to love and to look for joy in everything.

Finally, eternal and loving thanks for my wife, Brenda, for her patience, support, and especially her courage. She also performed the amazing feat of editing this book. Brenda is now a converted netizen and highly skilled researcher. She remains my heart and joy!

And at last, to the fine folks at Lassiter Starbucks for fueling this book with their endless African Blends.

---

[*] **Blogosphere** (alternate: blogsphere) is the collective term encompassing all weblogs, or blogs. Weblogs are heavily interconnected; bloggers read other blogs, link to them, and reference them in their own writing. Because of this, the interconnected blogs have grown their own culture.[9]

For my children, Ryann & Martin
Citizens of the Digital Age,

And for my Freshman Industrial Arts Teacher
Mr. Bill Edwards,

A facilitator of learning

Table of Contents

BUILDING A PROFESSIONAL (OR PERSONAL) BLOG   97

CLASSROOM BLOGGING WITH CLASS BLOGMEISTER   127

PODCASTING

APPENDIX

Introduction

At the turn of the century, teachers in classrooms across the U.S. and many other parts of the world were becoming acquainted with newly arrived multimedia computers and broadband access to the Internet. We were exploring new techniques for utilizing these seemingly magical tools to improve teaching and learning. We also recognized the importance of these technologies in preparing our children for what will surely be a future that is heavily influenced by computers and global networks. We explored a wide variety of new web-based instructional services and learned to build webquests[*] for our students, to provide rich inquiry activities to help students learn to use the Net to teach themselves and to use their growing knowledge and skills to produce new knowledge and valuable information products.

At that giddy time, none of us had heard of Blogs. If we had heard the term, it would have conjured up visions too uninteresting to want to know anything about it. Yet today, blogs[*] have become an important and influential force in politics, entertainment, art, religion, and many other aspects of modern society. As late as 2004, blogging was fairly limited to the techno-elite, with only a few suggestions of its potential importance emerging in likely places. My first blog experience was with a regularly updated blog called **Where is Raed?**. Published on a surprisingly steady basis, the author described daily events and details about life in Baghdad in early 2003, as U.S. troops massed along the borders of his country. As people in the U.S. and other countries watched CNN, listened to NPR, and read their favorite daily and weekly newsprint sources,

[*] **Webquests** are teacher-constructed online activities that provide a task for students to complete along with resources, context, and a described method for evaluation.

[*] A **blog** is an interactive web page most often used as a way to publish regular writings on a variety of issues and with a variety of goals. The term *blog* is a shortening of *Web Log*. It is sometimes referred to as a *weblog*.

many of them also tuned to **Where is Raed?** to learn about how the imminent invasion was affecting the residents of this far away country that had been so much in the news over the last decade.[1]

At that time, I had a conceptual understanding of what a blog was. I knew it as a way for almost anyone, regardless of technical expertise, to publish information for global audiences over the Internet. The process was not especially interesting to me. I had built a number of online tools for teachers that worked very much the same way, enabling them to publish content to their students and other classroom stakeholders, without having to know any HTML, FTP, XML, or sophisticated publishing software.

However, reading this particular blog began to move me beyond the concept of simple publishing technology toward understanding the potential impact of **giving voice to people like you and me**. One of the ideas that I will visit and revisit in this book is the importance and potential benefit of making our children part of…

The Great Discussion,

Today, the discussion is increasingly influenced and contributed to by nearly all walks of people, who observe, reflect, and report – a new society of *citizen journalists*.

…an ongoing public exchange and cultivation of ideas that was previously limited to hired and elected leaders, journalists, and pundits. Today, the discussion is increasingly influenced and contributed to by nearly all walks of people, who read and observe, reflect, and report – a new society of *citizen journalists*.

It was not lost on me that I did not know the author of **Where is Raed?,** nor was there an obvious way to research and prove his authenticity. However, when I *Googled*[*] the title of this popular blog, I immediately had access to 3,500 web pages that mentioned the blog. Of the ones that I examined, a vast majority were message boards where people were discussing just this issue – was the author really a citizen of Iraq living in Baghdad, or was he a college student in Kansas, playing the network. The point is that people were asking questions and talking about the publication's source, not just what was being written. They were seeking and discussing information about the information, rather than assuming the information's authenticity.

This points to another idea that will arise again in this book, that we must no longer assume the authority of the information we use, but, instead, be willing and able to prove its authority. This is a major shift that affects every teacher, learner, and classroom, not only in **what we teach our students**, but also **how we teach our students**.

..we should no longer assume the authority of the information we encounter, but, instead, prove the authority.

Continuing the story of **Where is Raed?**, *New York Times* journalist Peter Maass returned to the U.S. shortly after the invasion, and began to read the work of this "Baghdad Blogger," having returned to his home cable modem. As he read through the articles and other references to the author, he learned that Salam Pax, the author's pseudonym, had worked with an NGO called CIVIC, studied in Vienna, and worked as a translator for several foreign journalists. Peter Maass later reported in *SLATE Magazine*:

His latest post mentioned an afternoon he spent at the Hamra Hotel pool, reading a borrowed copy of *The New Yorker*. I laughed out loud. He then mentioned an escapade in which he helped deliver 24 pizzas to American soldiers.

---

[*] **Google**(v) – Google is the premiere search engine indexing web pages at the writing of this book. However, as a verb, to Google something means to take the word or term to the Google search engine and search the web for references within its 8,058,044,641 web page index.

I howled. Salam Pax, the most famous and most mysterious blogger in the world, was my interpreter. *The New Yorker* he had been reading—mine. Poolside at the Hamra—with me. The 24 pizzas—we had taken them to a unit of 82nd Airborne soldiers I was writing about.[2]

Blogs were later catapulted to our attention when Howard Dean ingeniously used the medium to attract millions of dollars in contributions for his presidential campaign. Writing a blog quickly became an integral part of political campaigning, and candidates without a blog were seen as behind the times and irrelevant. Blogging also surfaced as a prevalent avenue for reporting on campaigns. As more and more people are turning to the web for their news, and as publishing content to the web has become so accessible, it is only natural that blogging should become a force in how we use information to make our decisions.

It is difficult to claim that blogging, or any other single technology, seeded the appearance of something new, but the last two years have witnessed the emergence of a new family of web applications that are so changing the way that we think about information, that people are starting to call it Web 2.0. Blogging, podcasting, RSS, social networks, video conferencing, social bookmarks and others constitute a new information landscape where the web has moved beyond the digital library where we find and consume content, to an ongoing, constructive, inquiry and observation-driven online conversation, where people connect through their ideas.

During his junior year, my son started making videos with a digital video camera that he had bought the summer before working as a music camp counselor. But he was not merely taking video with his camera and then editing sequence. He was mixing in audio from the Internet, CDs and DVDs, video clips collected from friends, still images he had taken and downloaded from the net, and even staged video from online video games, where players followed direction and acted out scenes on a virtual stage from their homes across the globe.

I did not teach him how to do this. I know his high school teachers, and I know they did not teach him how to do this. He taught himself, with the help of his social network of people, with whom he IMs, text messages, shares MySpace pages, plays with in the metaverse of video games, and through venues I am sure I do not even understand yet. He knows how to use this new read/write web to learn what he needs to know, in order to do what he needs to do, now! It's how his generation learns. It's how they use information.

A Disruptive Technology

In 2004, I attended a *BloggerCon**, one of many conferences occurring across the U.S. and Europe, attended by practicing bloggers, blogger wannabes, and others who are directly concerned with this new avenue of communication. I had very little inkling of what to expect. I attend and work conferences for a living, and am quite familiar with how they operate. Participants attend various presentations to learn more about specific topics that are of importance or interest to them, listening to experts and learning.

I found that a BloggerCon is entirely different. Rather than a classroom arrangement, with a class leader and attendees politely listening, all of the BloggerCon sessions degraded into rather spontaneous, though mostly courteous, discussions. I knew that this was going to be different when blogging icon Dan Gilmore got up for the keynote address, and the first thing that he said was, "Any questions?"

I left entirely unsatisfied. However, I realized over the next couple of weeks that the conference kept coming back to me, reminding me of ideas I had heard and things I had learned from these conversations. I realized that it was, indeed, a useful and even a powerful learning experience, and that we

---

* **Bloggercon** – A meeting or conference of bloggers, where a variety of issues are discussed, but rarely settled. Most bloggercons are fairly local, addressing issues of blogging in a particular city or region.

were mirroring the act of blogging in those meeting rooms. All participants had equal voice, equal right, and equal opportunity to share their ideas, questions, and answers. As I now attend other blogger events, since realizing their format, I leave with a wealth of knowledge, and frequently write about them in my blog, *2¢ Worth* (http://2cents.davidwarlick.com/), so that my readers can share in my new knowledge and build on it – continuing the conversation and further educating me. I was learning without a teacher. Instead, I was learning within a community or network of teachers.

Within the context of this open learning conversation, certain contentions have appeared between bloggers and traditional journalists. It is logical that many journalists have resented the increased notoriety of bloggers as reporters of their experience, and that they should caution us (rightly) to be careful with the news we read in blogs. They point to the value of traditional sources of the news because of the practices that most news publishers and networks undertake to assure accuracy and objectivity. There are certainly instances when traditional journalism did not do its homework and inadvertently reported what was inaccurate and/or intentionally angled a story toward a particular side of the issue. Fact-checking bloggers have uncovered more than a few missteps by the fourth estate. Still, the news industry has a stake in preserving their reputation as a reliable source of information. So they have a right to distrust these new citizen-journalists, writing their blogs in bathrobes and slippers.

On the other side, bloggers aspire to a new environment where we all observe, reflect, and share, and where the reader has the right, and the skill, to make his own decision about the information he uses. One notable exception to this conflict between traditional journalism and the blogosphere is the *News & Record*, the daily newspaper of Greensboro, North Carolina. The editors of what is the sole source of daily print news for the citizens of North Carolina's Triad region decided early on to embrace the new publishing paradigm. They have even invited local citizens to blog about the news and include some articles in their print publication.

The paper's online version has taken on a general blog look, with many of the stories and all editorials appearing as blog articles. The editor's page is a blog, called *The Editor's Log* (http://blog.news-record.com/jrblog/). One of the principal blogger journalists in the country is Ed Cone, a reporter for this forward-looking newspaper.

Aside from the logical disruption between traditional and blog-based journalism, the growing blogosphere has been responsible for some major events in our national and international lives. Consider Trent Lott, once the most powerful man in the U.S. Senate, and now the only Senate Majority Leader ever to resign under pressure. It started when attending Senator Strom Thurman's 100th birthday party. Lott said, "When Strom Thurmond ran for president, we voted for him. We're proud of it. And if the rest of the country had followed our lead, we wouldn't have had all these problems over all these years either." Thurman had been an ardent defender of segregation. It was his signature issue. Lott **appeared** to be aligning himself with that issue.

Interestingly, the mainstream news did not pay attention, and did not report the statement. However, bloggers did, and as a result, the story came to light, eventually moving conservative writer David Frum to call Lott's words, "…the most emphatic repudiation of desegregation to be heard from a national political figure since George Wallace's first presidential campaign."[3]

In the following months, Eason Jordan, cofounder of *CNN*, and Dan Rather, resigned under pressure for misstatements and manipulative reporting under the watchful eyes of a growing number of fact-checking citizen journalists – bloggers.

For this and other reasons, blogs have become the *mot du jour*, recognized by Merriam-Webster as the 2004 **Word of the Year**, and bloggers identified as the **People of the Year** by *ABCNews*.[4] Dave Sifry, the CEO of Technorati, the Google of the blogosphere, recent said in his blog…

> Technorati is now tracking over 70 million weblogs, and we're seeing about 120,000 new weblogs being created worldwide each day. That's about 1.4 blogs created every second of every day.[5]

Simultaneously, more people are gaining access to broadband Internet, and able to download enormous amounts of information in the full spectrum of media (text, images, sound, and video). According to a recent Pew Internet in American Life report, by "..March 2006, 42% of Americans had high-speed at home, up from 30% in March 2005. "[6] The rate of broadband penetration is grown even faster in other countries where their access speeds are much higher than what we enjoy in the U.S.

Information & Literacy

Broadening the scope just a bit, the past several decades have seen a dramatic change in the very nature of information. Computers, microprocessor equipped entertainment appliances, the Internet and the World Wide Web, fiber optics, and increased access to information via wireless technologies have brought about a new information landscape, one that is relatively new to many educators, but all that most students have ever known. Video game developer and author Marc Prensky introduced us to a comparison that has been useful, as educators and education leaders attempt to retool our education system to our twenty-first century citizens. In his essay, by the same name, Prensky referred to our students as *digital natives*. They have grown up in this new information landscape, and they speak without an accent.

We, on the other hand, at least those many educators in our classrooms who are over 30 years of age, are *digital immigrants*. We were educated and spent much of our formative life before computers and the Internet had inserted itself into our cultural identity. For me, when I started teaching social studies, the desktop computer had not been invented. Computers had nothing to do with my notions of what it meant to teach or to be a teacher. I am a digital immigrant and I speak with an accent.

The information environment in which our students spend much of their time is substantially different from the one that we know, and it has affected how they seek entertainment, interact with each other, and how they learn. However, all things considered, there are only four things that can be said about information today that was foreign to the textbooks and lectures that I experienced when I was a student in the 1950s and '60s. Information today is increasingly:

- Networked,
- Digital,
- Overwhelming,
- And exists outside of containers.

Each of these new characteristics impacts on how we use information to accomplish our goals – our literacy skills.

For more than a century, the three-Rs have been a popular way of describing basic literacy skills – what children should be learning in school. Sir William Curtis, the Lord Mayor of London, coined the phrase in the early nineteenth century. Not an extraordinarily literate man himself, Curtis said that school must teach students the three-Rs: Reading, Riting, and Rithmatic. Our task today, as educators in the twenty-first century, is to rephrase literacy in light of this new information landscape; to redefine it so that the skills we are teaching our students reflect the information environment that will certainly be their future.

So, what does it mean to be a reader when information is increasingly networked? I was taught to read the text that was in front of me, and I rarely had access to information that was not filtered by editorship, publishing, and librarians. Today, I have access to billions of pages of information, much of it published directly to the web by authors with their own reasons for writing, and without any kind of filtering.

Reading expands into skills for Exposing the Truth

Reading has become a much richer and more interesting practice. It is no longer merely the ability to decode the text in front of you. Being a reader now requires skills in finding information within a global electronic library that is relevant to the task you are trying to achieve. It includes being able to decode the information regardless of its format (text, sound, images, video). It also requires the ability to evaluate the information to determine its value and to organize the information into personally meaningful and valuable digital libraries.

Arithmetic expands into a wide range of skills involved in Employing Information

Arithmetic does not go away in the twenty-first century. However, two things have happened in recent years that force us to expand what it means to be a processor of information. First of all, when we solve problems today with numbers, they are not a dozen numbers on a piece of paper. They are thousands of numbers, and they are digital. Therefore, the skills to use information to solve problems and accomplish goals must include the ability to access and process thousands of digital numbers.

The second change is that the range of process-able information has expanded. When I was in school, I was taught to process numbers. I learned a little bit of writing, but text was mostly for reading. Images were to view. Audio was for listening to and video was for watching. Today, all information is made of numbers. Images, sound, video, it's all made of one's and zero's. Because of the proliferation of numbers, it has become possible, and a basic working skill, to be able to process images, sound, and video for the purpose of adding value to the information.

Writing expands into skills involved in Expressing Ideas Compellingly

We all feel overwhelmed by information. E-mail, blogs, web searches that return millions of results, television, radio, instructions for operating our devices, and on and on. The fact is that we expend a great deal of energy to determine what information we are going to pay attention to, and what information we are going to ignore. As a result, the information that we use is that which successfully competes for our attention. In the information age, information must compete for attention in much the same way that products on a store shelf competed for attention in the industrial age.

In the information age, information must compete for attention in much the same way that products on a store shelf competed for attention in the industrial age.

In much the same way that we packaged store products to attract attention, information must also be packaged today. Information must not only look attractive, but it must look and be easy and efficient to use. As an example, a body of text that consists of a few long paragraphs looks more challenging to read than does a body of text comprised of shorter paragraphs with white space between. In the same vein, some information communicates itself more efficiently and more effectively as images. Some information conveys itself better as audio, or video, or animation. If we are teaching writing as a communication skill, then we should also be teaching our students how to communicate with images, with sound, with animation, and with video. It is the nature of information and our use of that information.

Ethics has become an explicit part of what we consider Literacy Skills

As information increasingly defines our activities, both as consumers and producers of content, its abuse can have an even more devastating impact on individuals and groups of people. Consider the financial scandals of 2002, when a handful of corporate executives at ENRON, WorldCom, Anderson Consulting, and Tyco, to mention only a few, brought the economy of the United States to its knees – by abusing information. We live off of information today. It is the infrastructure of our economy and much of our culture. The information infrastructure is no less critical to our survival and prosperity than our roads, bridges, and seaports. Abuse of the networks by malicious hacking, spyware and adware, viruses, and spam costs our economy billions of dollars a year in lost time and productivity and efforts to lock down the infrastructure and protect it from this onslaught. In schools, much of the benefit that could be gained from the millions of dollars worth of technology that we invest, must be crippled by blocking, filtering, and system lockdown procedures.

Our technological solutions imply that the problem is one of technology, when it is more a problem of our behavior. Most questions of information ethics today did not exist ten years ago, or they only existed to a very few people in the publishing and broadcast industries. The codes of ethical behavior that were espoused by journalists have become common codes of behavior for all of us, and they must become an integral part of any definition and any conversation about literacy in the twenty-first century.

What is important to us, as educators, is the direct and conspicuous relationship between blogging and literacy. Blogging is about reading, thinking, writing, and reading some more. It is about communicating. And through blogging and other Web 2.0 technologies students can be offered opportunities to learn through communication – within conversations. It has become their **learning literacy**. If we can tap into the sudden notoriety of blogging as a *cool thing to do*, giving our students authentic assignments of finding, reading, and evaluating blog-based information within the context of curriculum, and then make them bloggers, or communicators with a broadening audience, then we may do a more effective job of teaching literacy, both in the traditional sense, and within the context of an emerging new definition of literacy in a networked, digital, and overwhelming information landscape.

History of Blogs

I was a history teacher for nearly 10 years, and this background certainly has some bearing on my including a chapter on the history of blogs. Still, the history of a technology tells us much about its context, motivation, intended and unintended influences. These are perspectives that our students do not have, nor do they naturally think about. They have not lived long enough, witnessed enough, nor are they as aware of their broader heritage as my generation. They did not grow up during the golden age of TV.

In researching the history of blogs, I found that some references pointed to the 18th century as the beginning of the practice. There were no computers, the Internet ran on horseback, and electricity was little more than an object of parlor tricks. Yet something very similar to blogging was happening. A new class of literate citizens was rising in parts of Europe and in the American colonies. Coupled with the fact that paper was becoming much cheaper to produce and more plentiful, and printing presses and print shops were appearing in many sizable towns, people began to report their views in print and to publish them to wide audiences as *pamphlets*. Perhaps the most famous of the revolutionary pamphleteers (from a U.S. perspective) was Thomas Paine, whose publication of <u>Common Sense</u> had an enormous influence over my country's move toward independence.

As electronic media (radio and then television) emerged a century and a half later, a rift occurred between the production and consumption of information. To produce information required hundreds of thousands of dollars worth of equipment and highly trained technical staff. The rest of us worked our industrial age jobs so that we could afford the technology (radios and then TVs) that enabled us to receive and be entertained by the growing electronic media industry.

Then, during the last years of the 20th century, conditions occurred not dissimilar to that which gave rise to the pamphlets. Personal computers appeared that dealt with information as coded strings of ones and zeros – binary code.* This *digital** information could be processed in powerful ways with computers, and ultimately communicated globally and compellingly through the Internet, first through dial-up modems, then local and wide area networks, and today through increasingly ubiquitous broadband Internet.

In the early days of the World Wide Web, content publishers used arcane markup languages in order to format the information for effective reading. Later, more WYSIWYG* tools arrived enabling more people to publish content over the web in much the same way that we were using programs like Pagemaker to publish in print. However, these publishing tools were expensive and still required a learning curve in order to master the increasingly complex interface.

Finally, Content Management Systems* (CMS) appeared. These simple web management tools enabled people, with Web access, to add and edit information on their web pages merely by editing the text in a web form. Upon submitting the form, the content of the page was immediately updated. Many teachers and school administrators are using content management systems to maintain their classroom and school web sites. The important point was that communicators could now publish their ideas to a global audience with only the most

---

* **Binary Code** – Information that is expressed as numbers on a base-2 scale. Our math is based on ten digits (0,1,2,3,4,5,6,7,8,9). Binary is based on two, (0,1). Still, it works the same way. Counting to five in binary would read: 1,10,11,100,101. The new language also converts text to binary making the letter "a" a 65, "b" a 66, etc. Computers operate very efficiently using binary, and information is expressed very clearly.

* **Digital** refers to information that is coded in binary form, using ones and zeros. Any information can now be expressed as digital: numbers, text, images, sound, animation, and video.

* **WYSIWYG** stands for *What You See Is What You Get*. It refers to software that enables content producers to structure information on their computer screens to the look that they hope to accomplish in the final published work.

* A **Content Management System** enables web site managers to control the content of their site using web forms to enter and edit the text.

basic web navigating skills and any basic web browser. The stage was set, and waiting only for the visionaries to take hold.

It began with web pages that were created and maintained by individuals who made it their practice to monitor the Web, identifying new sites of value to their readers, and posting links and short descriptions in their web pages. Justin Hall started his "Filter Log" (http://www.links.net/vita/web/original.html) in 1994. Four years later, Jorn Barger coined the term "weblog" and Peter Merholz announced that it should be pronounced "wee-blog," later shortening it to *blog*, with weblog writers referred to as "bloggers."

In 1999, Blogger (http://blogger.com) and Pyra Labs (http://pyra.com) launched free web sites that enabled anyone to establish a weblog account and start their own weblog pages, simply by filling in web forms.[7] [8]

The rest is fairly common knowledge, except for the degree to which blogging is beginning to be integrated into the work place. Microsoft saw this phenomenon with its premier blogger, Robert Scoble, who freely talked about the Microsoft culture and linked to other employee blogs that talked about that near sacred world. Peter Quintas (CTO of Silkroad Technology) and Peter Kaminski (CTO of Socialtext), recently attended the American Cancer Society's Innovation Summit, where blogging was one of the major topics of discussion. Quintas and Kaminski reported in an *ITConversations* (http://itconversations.com/) published podcast that although most of the attendees were relatively inexperienced in the blogging process, there was an overwhelming sense that they recognized and were planning ways to use this new avenue for communication – to help them accomplish their goals. Consider the effects of encouraging colon cancer survivors to blog about their experiences, and linking their statements from official Cancer Society sites,[9] or encouraging students to blog about their learning experiences both inside and outside their classrooms.

As more teachers are starting to blog, education conferences have taken on new shape. Blogging educators attend presentations, in rooms that increasingly provide WiFi access to the Internet. They blog their notes and impressions from the seminars and workshops and post them to their blogs. Educators who are not able to attend these events can benefit from the postings of attending bloggers. In addition, learners at these conferences are becoming teachers. Professional development is becoming a conversation.

Finally, consider the growing video game industry, which has been drawing more revenue than motion pictures since 2002. Especially young people are being drawn away from the passive consumption of information, from TV and radio, by more interactive forms of entertainment. The player is participating in developing the plot of the story through his interactions with the game's information environment.

Often, however, players are putting aside the game company's intent, and inventing their own games, using the virtual environment and its capabilities and constraints to make new rules and new goals. Some people are using the game's environment as a movie set, directing the play of other teenagers over the Internet and recording the action and sound using video editing software that came preinstalled on their computers. Then they edit the captured game play into story plots that they share as video files over the Internet. J. Allard, Corporate Vice President of Microsoft, calls today's children the *ReMix generation*, because they access, select, and capture content, and then remix the content to suit their needs.[10] It is a generation that is at home in a new information landscape and expects to exercise control over the information and to use it to accomplish their goals. Blogging is a sublime expression of this mode.

Teaching, Learning, & Blogging in the Long Tail

At the point of writing this page, I am sitting in Starbucks at the Lassiter, in North Raleigh. I do much of my writing here, because it gets me away from the distractions of having e-mail and web surfing so easily available. My coffee comes free of charge, because educators who use one of my free online web tools periodically donate money into my Starbucks card, through the SB web site, as thanks for the free tool and my support.

When I need to send an e-mail or access a web page as part of my writing, I can pull out my mobile phone, a Motorola Q, which has a very fine web browser. As one final note, local to this personal time, my wife informed me as I was finding my car keys, that my son is averaging 78 text messages a day, now that he is away at university.

We certainly do not need any more evidence that the nature of information has changed over the past decade or so. Still, I would like to spend a few pages building a landscape for this new information environment that I think will not only help us to see the changes better as educators but also as life-long learners. This has much to do with blogging, but also the full range of Web 2.0 applications that give us so much access to so much information and the ability to participate in that information environment.

In 2004, Chris Anderson, the Editor in Chief of *WIRED Magazine*, wrote a blog entry reporting some conclusions he was drawing about data he had discovered and worked with over the months. He called his article, *The Long Tail,*[11] and it generated so much buzz on the blogosphere that he started a new blog by the same name. Anderson continued to research the concept of the long tail and to broaden its implications, tossing out a wide variety of insights about the new behaviors of information, generating more conversation.

In July of 2006, he published a book, in it describing at some length the experience of using his blog and its discussions as a research tool for writing the manuscript. Anderson centers on two basic pivot points around which information moves, both tied to the fact that information many of us grew up with, was made of atoms. It was letters, numbers, words, paragraphs, diagrams, and images that were stamped or scratched on paper, or some other physical surface that had to be carried from where it was produced to where it was read or viewed. So there were two limitations within which our information systems resided, geography and shelf space.

Growing up in a small mill town in western North Carolina, I had access to the books that could be stored on the shelves of the astonishingly large, well organized, yet limited library in that town. There was one record store in the town that probably offered, at any one time, not more than a thousand songs (mostly singles). The shelf space of that town was limited, offering me access to information that by today's standards was medieval.

Geography also played a part in the limitations of information, as there are no major publishing or recording facilities anywhere in my state, and the books that were available to me all came from less than a half-dozen places in the world. The physical transportation of that information impacted significantly on what I could read and listen to. Television and radio greatly improved my access to information as it turned the information into analog signals that could be transmitted a limited distance over the airwaves. We had four TV channels and probably no more than six or eight reliable radio channels.

Of all the text, audio, images, and video information in the world, most people had access to only a minute portion of that content because of geography and shelf space. The publishers and networks decided what information we would have access to based on evolving theories and models for what would be most popular, creating hits, blockbusters, and best sellers.

Today, the increasing digitization and networking of information has practically wiped out geography and shelf-space as limiting factors of how information behaves. Today, I am no long limited to the few thousand books available through the public library, but millions of books available through Amazon.com. iTunes gives me access to any wide or narrow genre of music in which I might be interested, and delivers the music immediately to my computer and then to my media player. I have access to hundreds of channels of television, but actually spend most of my viewing time watching DVDs that I order from the 55,000-file Netflix digital catalog. I choose the movie or DVD TV program I want to watch, and they ship it to me, usually the next day.

I am almost ashamed to say that I am now spending too much time watching YouTube (http://youtube.com), an online service that invites people, like you and me, to upload our own video productions. Most of them have very little value, but some have been so beautiful, or moving, or funny, that they have become the talk of the planet. And this is part of the point of the long tail. When geography ceases to mean anything in terms of shipping content, and shelf space is practically without any limits, then the range of content available to us grows as does opportunities for each of us to share our own stories.

So what is the tail? Anderson constructed a graph that illustrates the number of information products sold by a company or group of companies. In his original blog, he shared data on Rhapsody (music), Amazon.com (books), and Netflix (movies), producing a graph that plotted the products by the number of sales, generating a curve that one would expect, the blockbusters and best sellers at the top and trade books near the bottom. However, at a specific point, the curve leveled out, and it kept going and it kept going. This is the long tail. *(See Long Tail Diagram)*

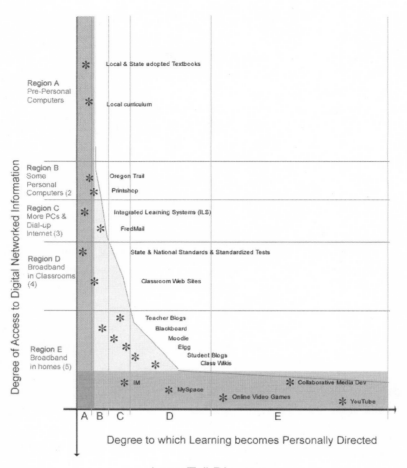

Long Tail Diagram

The products in the tall region are books, music, and movies that sold enough copies to be profitable to ship to stores. The books, music, and movies in the tail did not sell enough copies and they never could sell enough copies. Yet they are there, because of a new digital bazaar that operates independent of geography and shelf space, a place where you and I can market our own content. The long tail represents books, and music, and movies that didn't exist only a few years ago. It represents authors, musicians, composers, and filmmakers who were not engaged in those activities a few years ago.

The long tail offers a reason why we should be enriching what and how we teach to help our students to become skilled and responsible producers of information at the same time that we continue to help them become skilled and responsible consumers of information. But beyond that, what are the teaching and learning opportunities in the long tail? Before we dive more deeply into blogging and the other Web 2.0 applications, let's take a quick tour of the tail as educators.

Region A – Pre-Personal Computers

Referring to the Long Tail Diagram above, Region A, the narrow ribbon at the far left of the curve, is where most of us are comfortable. It represents the education that we experienced as learners, and for many of us, the education that we have spent much of our careers delivering. It is an environment that is ruled by geography and shelf-space. Because of limited shelf-space and the expenses of publishing books, textbooks are largely adopted at the state level (in the U.S.), with districts or schools having a choice within the limits provided by the state. We were largely limited to what information could be stored in our classrooms or carried in from places that were reachable with our sneakers.

As shelf-space provided for a highly centralized textbook system, geography made it difficult to establish and support curriculum on such a large scale. When and where I taught, our school had its own curriculum. We spent weeks every few years rewriting what and how we would teach. In the state I moved to, as a district level director of technology, there was a standard course of study, distributed then as a library of notebooks with goals and objectives for each subject and each grade level. We called them *the Great White Books*, and they were largely ignored as there was no way for the state to enforce or support the curriculum.

The top of the curve is a place for books, local (classroom) control, and rarely changing techniques for teaching and learning.

In moving down the curve, I would also like to trace a history of technology use in the classroom, beginning with textbooks and closed classrooms and moving through to our present information landscape – moving from an education system defined by its limits, to an education system defined by its lack of limits.

Region B – Some Personal Computers

In the late 1970's and increasingly in the early 80's, personal computers began to appear in classrooms. These 16 to 128 kilobyte monochrome computers did almost nothing to affect geography and shelf-space, though I used to boast that I could store a novel on a four and a quarter inch floppy disk *(if you don't know, don't ask)*. However, a few students and a few teachers had an opportunity to explore ways to produce content either through programming or rudimentary desktop publishing applications. Practically no curve happened during this time, though the few who were paying attention understood that one was on its way.

Region C – More PCs & Dial-up Internet

During the middle to late 1980's, a handful of educators began to see their classroom walls become invisible, as they started getting grants to buy modems for their computers and phone lines for their classrooms. They used a number of online services for finding and accessing content (Dialog, The Source, and CompuServ) and bulletin board services (BBS) for communicating between classes, and from country to country. Chief among these online BBSes was FrEdMail, established by visionary educators in the San Diego area (principally Al Rogers and Yvonne Andres). These innovative activities were rare, but practitioners were celebrated in the growing educational technology community.

Also at this time, Integrated Learning Systems (ILS) emerged that provided instructional activities for students, constantly customizing the lessons based on the learner's performance and mastery.

Neither of these activities resulted in much of a curve for education, though the ILS illustrated an amazing variety of learning experiences independent of shelf-space. At the same time, a growing number of people outside education were beginning to buy computers with modems, and to login to CompuServ and America Online to access content and engage in conversations. The curve started. The long tail began to sprout.

Region D – Broadband in Classrooms

Starting in 1995, the federal government began to invest in classroom technology. We began to see more powerful multimedia computers, and connectivity, largely due to NetDay, a program that called on local communities to volunteer their time and resources to run Ethernet cable to the classrooms, much of it donated by the emerging tech industry. Libraries started to subscribe to online services that gave students dramatically increased access to digital periodicals, reference materials, and sometimes to multimedia.

Many teachers built and maintained classroom web pages, and some began to add content to the tail by building and publishing WebQuests. Yet, little happened to alter what and how students learned. With more families buying computers and getting AOL accounts, and the burgeoning video game industry growing into a presence that would soon surpass the motion picture industry in revenues, the tail began to take shape as people had access to an amazing array of information experiences.

But not in schools.

Region E - Broadband in Homes

Entry into a new century saw a downturn in the educational use of technology, especially within the context of long tail behaviors. The focus of computer use shifted to basic skills and test preparation, and although some states created or maintained technology literacy programs, little was done to move schools into the tail that was in the process of spreading out into a nearly infinite array of information possibilities.

Still, the emergence of new *Web 2.0* applications provoked conversations among a growing number of edtech visionaries. Possibilities were revealing themselves through these conversations, and many educators began to experiment with applications like blogs, course management systems, education-based social networks, student blogs, and wikis. Although the tail remained almost non-existent for schools, people started to talk about one.

Outside of school, things were moving. Even though they were hampered by the dot-com bubble burst, these years saw the emerging growth of long tail giants such as Amazon.com, eBay, NetFlix, iTunes, flickr, and more recently the ballooning blogosphere. Web 2.0 remained difficult to define, and as a result, even more interesting.

Perhaps the most important driving force behind the growth of the long tail was the dramatic increase in broadband access in the U.S., and even more so in other parts of the world. It used to be said that using the Internet was like sucking peanut butter through a straw. People, sitting at home at their computers, connected to their cable or DSL modems, now have access to a fire hose of information, and the computing horsepower to make effective use of that information. Shelf-space is meaningless. The only distance is the 18 inches between your computer screen and speakers, and your personal experience.

And that demand began to be filled as Macintosh computers were being shipped with iMovie, a sophisticated video editing program. Windows followed close behind with Movie Maker. Then came GarageBand from the Mac, and people, especially youngsters, spending hours a day in tailless classrooms, were producing and publishing music and video for the long tail.

According to a recent Pew Internet in American Life report, 57% of Internet-using teenagers in the U.S. have produced digital content and made it available over the Internet. From the perspective of their digital, networked, and overwhelming information landscape, our students are more literate than we are. Our classrooms are flat. The teacher is no longer the sole holder of knowledge and wisdom. Facts are a mouse-click away, and our students can click it faster than we can. Schools remain flat against the Y-axis of the Long Tail *(see Flat Schools & Flat Classrooms)*, while our classrooms, full of students who are IMing at home, and inhabiting Tail hungry applications like MySpace, YouTube, and online video games, are flat against the X. The intersection is small. It is dangerously small.

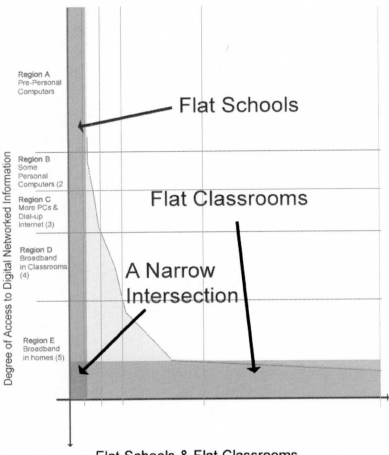

Flat Schools & Flat Classrooms

It is a major goal of this book to introduce the new web and the long tail to as many educators as possible, so that schools begin and continue to emerge into the tail and join our students there for meaningful learning.

Blogs & the Blogosphere

It is important to understand that although the blogosphere resides on the World Wide Web, it is different in some fundamental ways. The web has frequently been referred to as a large library – a global library. It is a fairly well indexed, nearly organized repository of formally published documents on nearly any subject you could imagine, and some you probably couldn't imagine.

In the same way that the web might be thought of as a global library, the blogosphere is a global conversation. Using the web has traditionally been an act of passively consuming information. Because of blogs, more and more Internet users are becoming active participants in the digital information environment.

...the blogosphere is a global conversation.

According to Dave Sifry, the CEO of Technorati, July 2006 saw 175,000 new weblogs created – each day. That is up from 38,000 blogs added per day when the first edition of this book was written. At that time, Bloggers were posting approximately 5.8 new articles every second. Today, it is up to 18.6 new postings a second.[12] This is content that is being added to the human knowledge bank, and it comes from people, observing their experience, reflecting, reporting, and engaging in conversations. Much of this content is of little or no use to any of us. However, there are serious people considering and reporting serious issues, and engaging in content-generating conversations – and this fact deserves our serious consideration as professional educators.

As with any other information systems, hierarchy is important. Some books are more important than others. Some magazines and journals have more influence, as do newspapers, composers, and film studios. If one were considering information about a current event, the *New York Times* would probably be more relied upon than a small town weekly. Assigning importance to blog content is one of the functions of the blogosphere.

A few years ago, using the web changed significantly because of one profound idea – that the relevance and importance of a piece of information should be based not on a single authority's judgment, but by the practices of many authorities. Much of the success of the Google search engine is based on the high quality of the web sites that surface to the top for our search results. These high relevance sites are based on a new but very simple idea. The importance, or relevance, of web sites is based not on how many times the search term appears in the web site or where it appears, but instead, Google ranks sites by the number of other related web sites that link to it – relevance by recommendation.

For instance, if you enter the term *euphonium* into Google you receive roughly 343,000 hits. The first page includes ten web links. In order to determine which web pages would be included on the first page, Google counted the number of other web pages that included the word *euphonium* and that linked to the pages. In this example, a web site called *Euphonium Net* surfaced to the top of the list. According to Google's link search trick,[*] 38 web sites link to *Euphonium Net*, including one German and two Korean sites.

If we go to the next Google page, the site listed at the top is *Euphonium Asylum*. Searching for other web sites that link to *Euphonium Asylum* (link:www.nikknakks.net/Euphonium) reveals only two sites. Therefore the judgment is made by

---

[*] If you want to see what web sites have web links to a page you are considering, type the URL of the site, without the prefix (http://) into Google. Precede the URL with the prefix, *link:*. Entering "*link:euphonium.net*" into Google lists 38 web pages that link to the site.

Google that *Euphonium Net* is more important to more people than *Euphonium Asylum*.

Technorati (http://technorati.com) works the same way. A search engine for the blogosphere, Technorati ranks blogs that include a key word by the number of other blogs that link to the considered blog.

Anatomy of a Blog

Now that we better understand the influence that blogging has had on our world, let's dive into what a blog really is. We will begin by dissecting a typical blog page and blog article, and then look at the process of blogging. Before we address some of these more technical aspects of blogging, it is important to understand that most of what you will be reading about in the following pages is handled by the blogging software or service that you use. Most of the time, you will simply type or paste your text into a web page form, and press a submit button to publish your latest blog publication. The technical environment takes care of most everything else for you.

First of all, blogs are personal. They are one way for an individual to express personal beliefs with a certain amount of personality. So there are probably as many ways that a blog can look and read as there are blogs. However, there are some fundamental features that most blogs have, each serving a purpose and helping the blogger to accomplish goals.

My own blog, *2¢ Worth* (http://2cents.davidwarlick.com), is typical in a lot of ways. First of all, it has a goal – two goals. First, my blog intends to help people understand the implications that our rapidly changing times have on what and how we teach our children. I also blog for the benefit of exposure to The Landmark Project.

So let's take a look at the anatomy of my blog and examine how it helps me do my job. I will point out the various features, and then discuss them on following pages *(see Anatomy of a Blog)*.

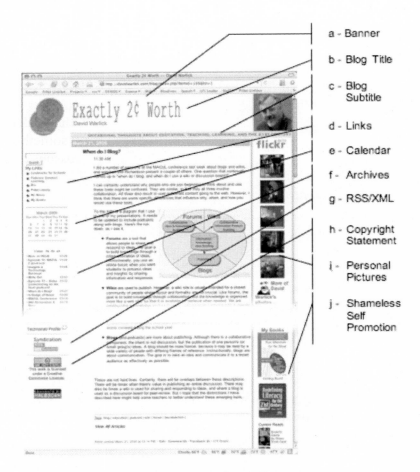

a - Banner
b - Blog Title
c - Blog Subtitle
d - Links
e - Calendar
f - Archives
g - RSS/XML
h - Copyright Statement
i - Personal Pictures
j - Shameless Self Promotion

Anatomy of a Blog

a. Almost all blogs have a **banner**. It is probably a holdover from print publishing and it solves a similar and important function. The banner establishes an over-all look for your blog page. It gives the page a unique identity. In the dot-com days, it was called *branding*. Current blog page style seems to advocate a minimal look without a lot of graphics and color. The focus is on content, and excessive use of graphics and color can distract the reader from the content. Also, in most cases, clicking the banner will take you to the front page, and most recent postings, of the blog.

b. A **Blog Title** is something that you should give some thought to. It is another way of distinguishing a bit of personality and creativity. I selected my title, *2¢ Worth*, because for years I closed many of my discussion and mailing list postings with that phrase, and the participants in those forums make up at least part of the readership of my blog. I wish that I had come up with something more clever. However, there are also lots of reasons to be less clever and more to the point. *Ms. Hobbleton's Classroom Blog* says it all.

c. The **subtitle** is a simple statement that describes the main focus of your blog. The statement of your subtitle should not excessively confine the topics that you blog about, but your article topics should logically point to your subtitle statement, and the statement should point logically to the topics and goals of most of your articles.

d. Many blog pages feature a list of **links** to web sites of particular value to the author within the context of the blog's goal. Many bloggers also include links to other blog authors whom they read. This is called a *blogroll*.

e. Many blogs include a **calendar**, notating each day that an article was added to the blog. I almost never use the calendar as a method of navigating a blog site. However, it does give us a good sense of how active a blog is.

f. An **archive** is an important part of a blog page. It is a list of the titles of past blog articles and it makes for an effective way for readers to find information that is most relevant to their needs and interests. This should be a consideration as you title your articles. They will soon appear in your archives list and they should be an effective pointer to information that readers are seeking.

Blogs should also include a search tool. This will enable users to find articles with specific keywords. Most blogging tools include a search feature.

g. We have not yet talked about **RSS** and **XML**. Part of this chapter will be devoted to the topic. Understand now that it is an important feature of a blog and helps regular readers of your publication to be notified when you have added or updated content. To calm any anxiety that two acronyms in one paragraph may have caused, RSS stands for *Really Simple Syndication.*

h. The **copyright statement** is also important, although all published information is automatically copyrighted under the Digital Millennium Copyright Act of 1998. Copyright has become a little more complicated, in that copyright law allows so few options (no options) in the kinds of rights that we may want to give to our content consumers. We will discuss Creative Commons later in this book.

i. It is important that blog pages avoid distracting the reader from your content. But **pictures** are fun and they do communicate. I use a service called flickr to store photos that I take with my camera phone, and it randomly inserts pictures that I have taken into my blog pages. More about flickr later.

j. People blog for many reasons and we all must make a living. As a person who is not traditionally employed, one of the reasons that I blog is to draw attention to my services so that people will consider hiring me to speak at their conference, or at least consider buying one of my books. Teachers should also use their blogs for **self-promotion**. You may not be working toward more employment, but it is essential in this day as education continues to come under attack, that we reassert ourselves as experts in a field that is of critical importance to the survival and success of our way of life. Use your blog to remind people that we are intelligent, educated, dedicated professionals and that we take our jobs seriously.

An additional feature that you do not find on my blog, but does show up on many others, is **Google AdSense**. There are other companies that provide the same service, but it is important to understand how this works in order to understand how and why some people blog. The blogger sets up an account with Google AdSense describing to a limited degree the content of their publishing. Google AdSense then generates some web code that the blogger copies and pastes into their template (a file that determines the layout of the blog page).

From that point on, Google is notified each time a reader loads your blog page. It examines the content of the page, and starts to create a profile of the content themes included in your blog, and selects advertisers from their database of thousands of companies whose products are related in some way to what you write about. After several days, the matches between the ads and your blog topics become surprisingly related, and Google pays you a few fractions of a penny every time one of your readers clicks one of the ads for more information. For most bloggers, this would amount to a little change each month. However, some bloggers enjoy a large enough readership that they are actually making a living through this search engine's advertising scheme. Essentially, individuals are becoming personal publishing companies, writing what people want to read, and generating income through advertising – selling *attention* to Google – all in their bathrobes.

Individual blog articles have their own sense of anatomy. Blogging is not merely an action of publishing information. Like the World Wide Web, blog articles are interconnected in several ways, creating a webbed archive of what people observe and what they think about it. The blogosphere is a multidimensional information environment, in which people are participating in new and rich conversations.

Because of this interconnectedness, it is important that blog content include some common features or conventions. Remember that most of these features are created and added by your blogging tool. We are merely going to learn what they mean and how they work.

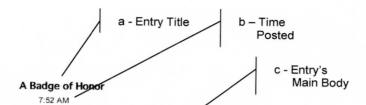

a - Entry Title b – Time Posted

c - Entry's Main Body

A Badge of Honor
7:52 AM

A while back, Steve Dembo, of Teach42, and I did a joint podcast about A.D.D. (Attention Deficit Disorder). We had discovered that we were both afflicted with the problem through our e-mail correspondence (ADDers can usually   so we inteviewed each other through iChat AV and St   d the interview as a Teach42 podcast. Two podcasts for the price of one!

d - Citation

The conclusion that we both came to, as a result of our talk, was that A.D.D. did have a flip side that gave us some advantages under certain conditions. I don't know what creativity is. It seems like some magical knack that some people have. To me, it's just having a mind that doesn't travel in a straight line. Ideas float around and seem almost repelled by each other, resisting my lining them up into a correctly bubbled in answer sheet.

However, I do easily see patterns in those ideas floating around, and when I describe those patterns, it's said to be creative. It's just a better way of thinking. It has served me quite well, that and the fact that I was smart enoug^   used business major.

e - Tags

What brought this up was an article that Ian Jukes pointed mt too in his blog, The Committed Sardine.

> Sam Grossman grew up thinking he was stupid, lazy and irresponsible?"a screw-up,"as he puts it. Struggling with attention-deficit/hyperactivity disorder (ADHD), he constantly disappointed his parents and teachers alike. So how, at the age of 24, did he end up as a partner in a Massachusetts real-estate firm? He credits an unlikely source. "The key to my success," he says, was his ADHD.

Jukes, Ian. "The Gift of ADHD?." The Committed Sardine Blog. 13 Mar. 2005. InfoSavvy Group. 20 Mar. 2005
<http://homepage.mac.com/iajukes/blogwavestudio/LH2004120111Ø546/LHA20050313225350/index.html>.

Tags: A.D.D. | education | IanJukes | technology | DavidWarlick | SteveDembo |

View All Articles

Article posted March 20, 2005 at 07:39 AM: • Edit • Comment (1) • Trackback (0) • 365 Reads

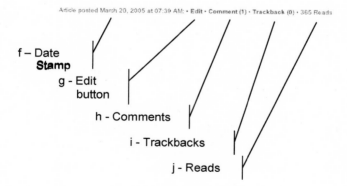

f – Date Stamp

g - Edit button

h - Comments

i - Trackbacks

j - Reads

Anatomy of a Blog Article

Referring to *Anatomy of a Blog Article...*

a. The **title** of your article is important mostly because it will appear in your archive and be used by readers to locate articles of interest to them. Titles should be short but descriptive. They should also be free of any HTML formatting *(more on that later)*.

b. The **time stamp** of an article's posting is included in the tag line at the bottom (or top) of the article. However, I will frequently add content to a day's blog article as the day goes on, so I will usually include the current time for that particular piece of information.

c. The **body** of the entry is the message itself. My articles are usually fairly long in comparison to others. It depends completely on your message and what you are trying to accomplish with your blog and this particular article.

    The body can include formatting and this is encouraged, as bulleting, indention, and images can help convey the message you are writing. Most blogging software includes formatting bars that allow you to control the text in much the same way that you would with a word processor. Some blogging software still requires you to enter some HTML code to format text. *(More about this later.)*

d. It is essential to treat a blog publication like any other writing, with regard to copyright. If you are using material from another source, even if it is another blog, then the source should be **cited**. I use Citation Machine (http://citationmachine.net/), to generate my MLA or APA citations. Other citation generators are also available.

e. More will be said about **tags** later. At this point, it is important to understand that tags are search terms that the author includes. Software on the Internet can link blog articles together by the tags that they carry. This means that an article I might write about No Child Left Behind, where I use *NCLB* as a tag, could automatically be linked to other articles about the education legislation. Not all blogging tools support tags, but there are ways to include them without the tool's assistance. *(More about this later.)*

f.   The **date stamp** is posted by the blogging tool when the article is initially posted. It is an official date for the blog entry and will be used in creating a chronologically sorted archive.

g.   The **edit** button allows the blogger to change or update a given blog entry. The button is password protected, so that anyone who clicks it must know the blogger's password to make changes.

h.   Most blogs include **commenting**. Readers, who wish to react to a blog article can click the 'comments' link and enter their ideas. Comments can be deleted by the blogger if they are not appropriate. The deleting of comments is a rather controversial issue. But in education, it is a necessary literary evil.

i.   If someone decides to write a blog article about your entry rather than post a comment, they can link their article to your entry using **trackback**. If four people have linked to your article using trackback, then the number four (4) will appear. You can click the link to receive links to those four blog articles. This is an important part of how the blogosphere is becoming a web of conversation and it is increasingly being done automatically by the blogging software.

j.   This is another feature that is not common. Your **reads** indicates the number of people who have looked at your article on your page. This number can be somewhat understated since more and more people are reading blogs through Aggregators. More about aggregators later.

The Blog Process

The process of blogging is amazingly simple and entirely unimpressive. In fact, this is what distinguishes blogging from the traditional process of publishing content to the web. There are essentially three steps.

1. Write your article.

2. Go to your blog submit page, paste your article into the textbox, and submit it.

3. Read and respond to comments.

Let's walk through the process with some pictures using Blogger, a commonly used blogging tool that is free and easy to set up. *(More about that later.)*

In step one, I have decided to write an article about music in education. I write blog articles in the text processor that came with my computer, TextEdit. Using this program is beneficial because it is lean, loads fast, has a spell checker that flags misspellings as I type them, and it has a speech tool that will read the text back to me. I find the speech feature especially useful since I will often hear awkwardness in my wording that is not apparent when I am reading my own text. The most important thing to have access to when you are writing is a spell checker.

When I have written, listened to, and edited the text of my article, then I go to the blog site (http://blogger.com). After loading blogger.com, I log in with my userid and password, and then click the blog I want to add an article to. *(You can have more than one blog with a single Blogger account.)* The blog's dashboard appears, which is like the dashboard of your car, featuring all of the controls and information you need to operate the blog. I rarely use any of the features here, except for **Post**. I click <Post> and then <Create> to add my article.

A page appears that asks for the title of the article and the text *(see Blogger Dashboard)*. I either type or paste the title from my text processor to the title textbox, and then the article. Blogger offers a variety of formatting tools that I can use to help my message communicate itself better.

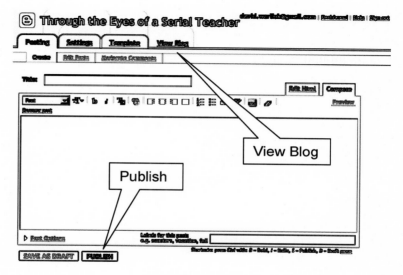

Blogger Dashboard

Finally, I click <**Publish**>. This adds the article to my blog, and clicking the <**View Blog**> button at the top will display my page with the new article at the top.

That is pretty much it. The article is available for reading and commenting. You can also edit the article if you want to add content, reword some text, or cut it out altogether. If someone wants to comment on an article, or you want to read comments, click the **\<Comments\>** link in the tag line and the page appears.

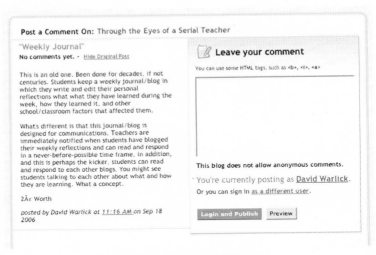

Blogger Comment Page

As I said before, one of the distinguishing characteristics of blogging, and perhaps the most important reason that it has grown at unprecedented rates, is the ease in which people can publish their ideas. Write, paste, submit.

RSS & Aggregators

At the same time that blogging is easy enough for most first graders and senior citizens, it is important to note that some pretty fancy stuff is happening in the background. For instance, because of RSS, powerful information functions are possible that make the blogosphere come almost to life.

One of the original problems experienced by early readers of blogs was that following five or more bloggers became difficult when you had to visit each of the blog web pages each day to see if any of them had a new article. This was a time-consuming endeavor and most people simply did not take the time to visit the same web pages every day.

Enter RSS. This acronym stands for something so esoterically technical that no one remembers what it is. Most people refer to it as *Really Simple Syndication.* This may well be the most complicated thing that we cover in this book, so go get a cup of coffee and sit down to learn how the nature of information is changing.

Let's try to get the geekie stuff over with quickly. When I pressed the submit button to add my new article to the blog, it did not just make a new blog page. It also generated a parallel document that listed information about all of my blog articles in a machine-readable code called XML. The XML file is not intended to be read by people, and most browsers now hide the file in its native format by formatting it for near-human consumption *(see XML File).*

```
<?xml version="1.0" encoding="UTF-8"?>
<!-- generator="wordpress/2.0.2" -->
<rss version="2.0"
    xmlns:content="http://purl.org/rss/1.0/modules/content/"
    xmlns:wfw="http://wellformedweb.org/CommentAPI/"
    xmlns:dc="http://purl.org/dc/elements/1.1/"
    >

<channel>
    <title>2 Cents Worth</title>
    <link>http://davidwarlick.com/2cents</link>
    <description>Occasional thoughts about education, teaching,
        learning, &#038; the 21st century</description>
    <pubDate>Thu, 19 Apr 2007 13:32:17 +0000</pubDate>
    <generator>http://wordpress.org/?v=2.0.2</generator>
    <language>en</language>
        <item>
        <title>The New M.B.A.?</title>

<link>http://davidwarlick.com/2cents/2007/04/19/the-new-mba/</link>

<comments>http://davidwarlick.com/2cents/2007/04/19/the-new-mba/#
comments</comments>
        <pubDate>Thu, 19 Apr 2007 13:32:17 +0000</pubDate>
        <dc:creator>Dave</dc:creator>
```

XML File

XML documents can be sniffed out (so to speak) by special software, enabling the content of the file, and consequently your blog articles, to automatically be linked into the blogosphere and indexed by blogging search engines *(such as Technorati)* – and it happens very quickly. This is important, since blogging, at its best, is a conversation, and conversations are immediate. It is critical that your statement becomes part of the conversation as quickly as possible.

The other benefit of this XML file is one more bothersome word I must introduce – *Aggregators*. Perhaps the best way to introduce aggregators is to show you one. The most commonly used example is Bloglines (http://bloglines.com), a web site with aggregator software operating in the background.

Here is one scenario on how you might use Bloglines. You are a science teacher, preparing a new unit on astronomy, and you would like to include some information about recent discoveries made by the Cassini Space Craft. You visit the Technorati web site and search for *cassini* and *saturn*. The search engine returns access to more than ten thousand blog entries.

You click one of the leading articles, *Surprise at Enceladus*, and read about a current mystery in the Saturnian system with one of its moons apparently holding an atmosphere when it is much too small to have sufficient gravity to do so. This is good information, because you learned long ago that current mysteries in science gets the attention of students.

You click the title of the blog site, *Centauri Dreams*, displaying the entire blog, where you can scan other articles in the weblog, and you recognize it as a rich source of regularly updated content that can help you with your unit. One last question, "Is the author an authority in terms of how you plan to use the information?" This is easy enough to determine. Open a new tab or web window and Google the author. To your delight you catch over 27,000 hits for Paul Gilster, and learn that he is a successful writer on topics of technology, digital literacy, and space exploration.

Now comes the RSS. You are not merely interested in what Gilster has written on one day, but also, in an ongoing effort to remain knowledgeable about the latest information on space exploration, you want to keep track of what this author writes in the future. On the Centauri Dreams blog page, you see a small orange button *(see Centauri Dreams RSS Link)*. Rather than clicking the button, you right click on the button, and select **<Copy Link Location>** or **<Copy Shortcut>**.

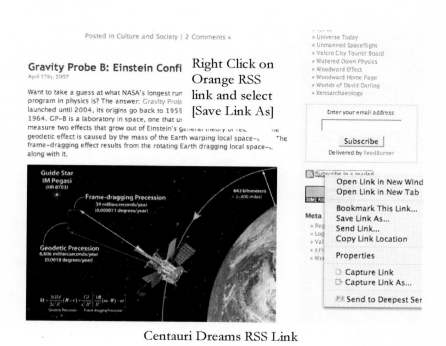

Centauri Dreams RSS Link

Now return to your Bloglines page and make sure you are logged in. Click the **<Add>** button (a) at the left, where the blogs you are paying attention to are listed. A textbox appears to the right asking for the blog or feed URL. Paste the link or shortcut here, and click **<Subscribe>**.

The Display Options allow us to decide if we want Bloglines to display entire articles, article summaries, or titles only. You can also apply this blog to a folder, or create a new folder.

Bloglines also has a downloadable notifier program that will produce a tone when Gilster publishes a new article. You have an option, here, to turn that feature on or off for this particular feed. There are other options that will probably not apply to us. But finally, you can add comments about the blog for later reference.

Clicking <**Subscribe**> will take you back to the Bloglines main page, with a panel to the left displaying the name of Paul Gilster's blog and any others you have subscribed to.

There is a much easier way to add blogs to your Bloglines aggregator. Near the bottom of the left panel, where your subscribed blogs are located, you will find a list of special features. Click <**Easy Subscribe Bookmarklet**>. A new page appears to the right with instructions for adding a bookmarklet. This process will plant a links bar of your browser, one of the toolbars common on most web browsers. The effect is a nearly one mouse-click subscription to a blog you wish to track. You simply load the blog, and click your new <**Sub with Bloglines**> link in your link bar. A page loads that captures RSS feeds or links included in the blog. Usually there is only one, but there can be more. You can click the <**Preview This Feed**> for each one to see the listing – but usually the first one listed will work well. Simply click <**Subscribe**> and then click <**Subscribe**> again, unless you are storing your listings in folders, and you have successfully subscribed to the blog. In review,

1. You load the blog,
2. Click your <**Sub with Bloglines**> bookmarklet,
3. Select a feed,
4. Click <**Subscribe**> and click the next <**Subscribe**>.

Perhaps the most important thing that Bloglines and other aggregators do is to keep track of your reading. When you load and login to the web tool, it automatically goes out to each blog page to which you have subscribed, and checks for new articles that have been added since the last time you viewed the entries. Beside the blog title in your listing panel, a number will appear, indicating the number of articles you have not read. Your aggregator will continue to periodically check all blogs you have subscribed to, keeping you connected to **the conversation**.

When you click the blog title, the unread articles will appear in the main panel. You may be able to scan or read the entire article, a summary of each article, or the titles only, depending on how you set up the feed. Clicking the title will link you to the original blog page.

See my Bloglines Feeds *(to the right)* to view some of the blogs and other sources that I have subscribed to with my Bloglines account and the number of articles I have not read. I actually do not use Bloglines as my primary aggregator, but instead use Google Reader (http://google.com/reader/), because it has a mobile phone version that I use at airports.

Bloglines Feeds

Aggregating the News

In 2004, I was asked to deliver a keynote address for the SETT conference in Glasgow, Scotland. The conference would be attended by technology-using educators and education leaders throughout Scotland and other parts of the U.K. I realized, about three months before the conference that I would need to know something about education there; its challenges, goals, programs, and relevant events. To accomplish this, I found the web site for *The Scotsman*, their capital newspaper in Edinburgh.

I discovered that the paper published its stories in print and on their web site. I was also surprised and very pleased to learn that they were also publishing their stories as blog entries, and their blog was RSS syndicated. So all I had to do was load the page that described their blog and listed the RSS feeds for the various sections of the page, *Education* among them, and then click my **<Sub with Bloglines>** bookmarklet. It listed all of the feeds; I found the one for education and subscribed. For the next three months I was notified each time a new story appeared in the Scotsman about education, and I arrived more informed and less naive than I would otherwise have been.

Most large newspapers and news magazines have RSS feeds for their news, as do many smaller publications. Even TV and radio are now offering feeds for podcasts. But more about that later.

To illustrate the use of feeds, let's look at the *New York Times*. You can load the *New York Times* web site (http://nytimes.com) and then click **<Add New York Times RSS Feeds>** near the bottom of the page. This will load a page that lists sections of the daily newspaper, including business, education, health, international, national, New York, obituaries, science, sports, technology, Washington, arts, automobiles, books, dining and wine, fashion and style, home and garden, job market, magazine, movie news, movie reviews, real estate, theater, travel, and subsets of many of these broader topics. Simply subscribe to the feed you like, and the news comes to you.

Creating an Ongoing News Search Feed

Receiving updated news on a broad subject can be very useful for a practicing teacher. However, most of the time we are searching for specific news on a specific topic that we are preparing to teach. Imagine being able to conduct a news search on the topic you will be teaching next month, then having the news search service continually make that search for you, and periodically inform you, through an RSS feed, as new stories appear.

Again, let's say that in developing a unit on astronomy, we have decided to use current and recent information about the Cassini Saturn Mission. If we could create an ongoing search through hundreds of news sources for articles related to the Cassini spacecraft and its mission, and then have it create an RSS feed based on the emerging results, and we could subscribe to that feed with our aggregator, then we would have a particularly useful and dynamic information source that would help us do our jobs.

The ability to create news feeds was pioneered by Justin Pfister, a web developer and programmer. Pfister reasoned out a way of sending a search phrase into Google's news service (access to hundreds of world-wide news sources), and generating an RSS feed that continued these searches, reporting new stories to your aggregator.

Search Tuning Box

Google has since integrated this feature into their News Search service. When you visit Google News (http://news.google.com), and type *cassini* and *saturn*, the search service finds 167 sources. In the Search Tuning box to the left you will find a link labeled RSS. You can subscribe to this link with your aggregator, and keep informed about the latest news on the topics you teach. Your students will be impressed and it is a perfect way to help with your efforts toward life long learning.

Other Types of Information that are being Expressed through RSS

We have looked at how blogs, as a source of valuable information, can be managed using RSS. News is also being made increasingly available through RSS to our aggregators. But any information that expresses value through its updates can be communicated through these esoteric but potent XML files.

When I teach workshops or speak at conferences, I make my handouts available through a blog. By subscribing to this blog, clients and potential clients can keep track of what I am teaching, and to whom. Since most of my presentations involve technology in some way, there are always lists of web sites included. Participants can link out and learn more about a particular issue by using these pages. As time goes on, I find new web sites on the topics I teach, and, using RSS, I can have them automatically added to all of the relevant online handouts. More on this later. These lists also feature RSS feeds that can be subscribed to by participants of my events, having the new web sites come directly to their aggregators.

I will have much more to say about online handouts as dynamic documents later.

Why is RSS Important?

For more than ten years we have increasingly relied on the web as a source of information, using tools like Yahoo, Alta Vista, and Google to go out and find information that helps us accomplish our goals. Today, that picture is changing dramatically, and it has only been going on for a couple of years. I continue to be thrilled by these developments.

Traditionally (if *traditionally* can be used when talking about the Internet), we have used search engines to find the information. Today, with RSS, we are starting to train the information to find us. It is radical and dramatic, and it adds one more element to what it means to be literate within a networked, digital, and overwhelming information landscape.

Yesterday, we used search engines to find information. Today, with RSS, we are training the information to find us.

I was taught to use tables of content, indexes, and alphabetical arrangements of information in reference books. My children taught themselves to Google for the answer to their questions. RSS, though it does not replace libraries and search engines, is much more powerful and personal. It facilitates continuing searches and delivery of content. It also requires us to be more active and deliberate in how we access information. Finding the information now involves skills in creating and cultivating personal digital libraries (our bookmarks and aggregators) where information literally presents itself to us. That information makes little sense to us if it does not appear within a contextual structure that makes sense. Librarians should rejoice, because library science has just become a "basic skill."

Librarians should rejoice, because library science has just become a "basic skill."

Consider RSS one more way. The World Wide Web, as we know it now, has been with us for 15 years. Its landscape was formed by the content that web masters put there. The roadmaps that we follow to navigate that information landscape were also laid out by web masters. They have done a very good job of building a revolution in information that reshapes the world.

Today, however, we are beginning to build our own roadmaps using RSS and aggregators. We are identifying the sources of information that are especially valuable to us and having that information updated directly to our points of need, within a context that we design. Things are changing, and that is what is exciting about being a teacher today.

Other New Web Digital Publishing Avenues for Teachers

Education is about communication. We help our students to learn by communicating with them. We teach them by orally expressing content and processes. We communicate visually with white boards, and increasingly with well-designed multimedia presentations and course management systems. We communicate with text and images through textbooks and other supplemental materials, and in many cases through web sites and CD-ROMs provided by textbook companies. Teachers also use communication to continue to improve themselves professionally by conducting ongoing research in their fields, engaging in professional discourse, publishing and reading.

As people have become more literate and sophisticated in their information skills, success increasingly depends on effective communication between teacher, curriculum, and student; the classroom and the home; and the school and its community. The community must become a partner in the education of its children today, in a way that was not important in the industrial age. Today, communication is the basic skill.

Today, communication is the basic skill.

It is important for educators to make note of who is using the Internet as a source of information today, and how they are using it. Although teens still dominate in using interactive applications (online games and IM), virtually every other demographic has increased in its use of the Internet, and especially in adoption of broadband access in the home. According to a 2006 PEW Internet in American Life Project (http://www.pewinternet.org/) report, broadband access grew by 40% from March of 2005 to March of 2006. Growth was especially dramatic among demographics that have traditionally been slow to adopt technology, including a 121% increase for African American families, 70% increase for households with less than a high school diploma, and 63% for seniors.[15]

Dr. John Horrigan, also of the PEW Internet & American Life Project, shared with an audience at OTX Research, a breakdown of American adults at various age levels who make regular use of the Internet. As you examine the Age Breakdown Graph, you will notice that the ages with the highest percent of users are from 18 to 44, peaking between 25 to 34 year olds.[16] Of importance to OTX (a technology firm that supports real estate and mortgage industries) was the fact that these age groups are new home buyers. Of importance to us is that these Internet users are the parents of our students.

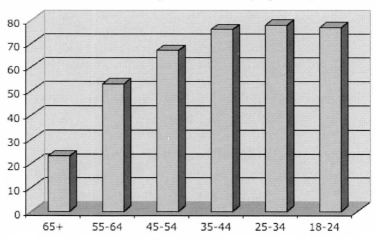

Age Breakdown Graph

A growing number of parents are using the Internet as a major source of information. If these trends continue, the Internet could soon be their preferred source, and they will expect to have online access to information about their children's education experiences. They will expect it to be rich and interactive. They will expect ongoing digital conversations with the people who are entrusted to prepare their children for the future.

As professionals who make their living by communicating, teachers should be using the World Wide Web as one of their avenues of communication. However, this does not mean that teachers should become web administrators *(Webmasters)*. They do not have time and it is not part of their job description. However, communicating is part of the job, and the information environment within which we communicate today is digital and it is networked. It is the Internet.

There is good news for stressed and beleaguered teachers. It has never been so easy to create and maintain classroom web sites. We have already mentioned Content Management Systems (CMS). The concept is simple and exceedingly powerful.

Content Management Systems

The distinguishing characteristic of content management systems (CMS) is that they are web sites that are built and updated by supplying information to a web form on a web page. It is:

1. Easy to do, and

2. Can be done with almost any standard web browser.

CMSs involve template web pages that include the visual elements that will appear on every page in the site. This can include the banner, footer, school or institution name, and main menu. The rest of the information is stored in a database that may or may not be installed on the web server computer. See the CMS Process for an illustration.

There are many examples of CMSs. In fact, most blogs are *content management systems*. You type or paste your article into a web form, hit submit, and your article becomes part of the blog site. It is actually stored in a database, and the blog page is assembled on the fly (pulling the standard elements from the template and databased content together) each time the page is accessed.

Many schools and school districts are also using CMSs for their school and classroom web sites. Some have built their own systems; others have contracted with local web developers to build them. Several companies also offer the service off of their own web server for a fee.

A teacher opens the edit version of a web page into a browser. This usually requires a login and password.

↓

The web server finds the information associated with that web page in the database and inserts that information into the web form of the edit page.

↓

The teacher enters, edits, or deletes some of the inforation in the web form.

↓

When the teacher submits the form, the updated information is inserted back into the database, replacing the earlier version.

↓

A student or parent accesses the public version of the page into a browser.

↓

The web server assembles the dynamic (databased) into the template page, and deliveries it to the reader's browser.

↓

The web server finds the information (just updated) assciated with that page in the database.

CMS Process

Wikis

One example of content management systems is the wiki, which is almost as exciting as blogs, and may be more interesting. Surprisingly, the wiki was first invented in 1995, by Ward Cunningham, a software engineer in Hawaii. He needed a quick way for a small group of people to collaborate in building a web document, so he developed a type of web site where users could click an **<Edit>** button, and then easily edit the content of the page. Rather than call his invention the quick web, he called it the Wiki Wiki Web, since *wiki wiki* is the Hawaiian term for quick. The label has since been shortened to wiki.

A wiki is a content management system, in that the content of the web pages are stored separately, and the pages are assembled on the fly as people access them. Wikis are, however, extremely open, in that many people (and in some cases, anyone) can contribute content to the site, edit the content, and grow the site as a living document. Most wikis are intended for in-house digital document development, where a small group of people is working together to grow and maintain a document. However, wikis can be wide open. The classic example is the *Wikipedia*, an online encyclopedia that owes all of its content to people who voluntarily add and edit articles. This collaborative online encyclopedia has grown at an astounding rate, more than four-and-a-half million articles at this writing, and it has remained amazingly accurate and reliable. We will explore the *Wikipedia* in more detail later in the book.

Like blogs, wikis are designed for ease of use. Perhaps the most popular wiki engine for educators is Wikispaces, a company that has made their service available for free to educators. You can set up and start building your wiki in only a few minutes.

Setting Up a Wikispaces Wiki

1. Go to the Wikispaces page to learn more about the service for teachers:

   http://www.wikispaces.com/help+Teachers

2. Go to the special registration site for teachers:

   http://www.wikispaces.com/site/for/teachers100K

3. Scroll down the page until you see a pastel green section, and begin filling in the form. Create a username for your account, make up a smart password, and enter your e-mail address. Finally, enter a name for your space *(3 to 32 letters, numbers, or hyphens)*, and then click the **<Join>** button.

   Tips for Username:

   First and middle initials and last name usually work, though it can be helpful to include number, such as birth date *(i.e. dfwarlick1030)*.

   Smart Passwords:

   1. At least six characters
   2. Must not appear in any dictionary
   3. At least one number
   4. At least one punctuation or symbol *(#, &, $, etc.)*.

4. I entered *jjjones* as the username in my registration. Wikispaces then returned a note that the username was already in use and suggested that I add a number to it. I added my birth date, making the username *jjjones1030*.

5. I will need to re-enter the password to complete my registration, then need to make special note of the section of the form that is returned called *Space Visibility*. There are three options:

   a. Public – This means that everyone can view and edit your pages.

b. Protected – If selected, everyone will be able to view pages, but only members who have been invited can edit the pages.

c. Private – Only invited members of the space can view or edit the pages ($5/month fee).

It would make the most sense to choose the second option. This would give you a wiki that students, parents, other teachers, and the community could view. You could also invite selected or all students to be able to edit your wiki, if you want to delegate responsibilities.

Some teachers have set up a second wiki space, setting one for students to be able to edit and one that only the teacher can edit. Wiki pages from different spaces can be linked to each other.

6. You now have a wiki, with it's own wiki space name. The URL of your wiki will be the wiki space name dot wikispaces dot com:

http://wikispacename.wikispaces.com/

or

http://jjjones-wiki-web.wikispaces.com/

7. Default content appears in your wiki page with 'instructions for getting started' information about Wikispaces. There are also a number of tabs that you can use to manage your wiki space:

Wiki Managing Tabs

a. **Home** – will return you to the home page of your wiki space.

b. **Edit This Page** – will return the content of the current wiki page within a WYSIWYG editor.

c. **Page** – returns you to the public view of the current page.

d. **Discussion** – provides a web form that will allow readers to post comments on the wiki page.

e. **History** – lists every time that the wiki has been edited. Earlier versions of the page can be reinstated as the current version.

f. **Notify Me** – provides a way for the reader to be notified of changes in the wiki page by e-mail or by RSS feed.

8. To start adding content to your wiki page, click the **<Edit This Page>** tab. The next page displays a picture of the edit box and the functions of some of the buttons.

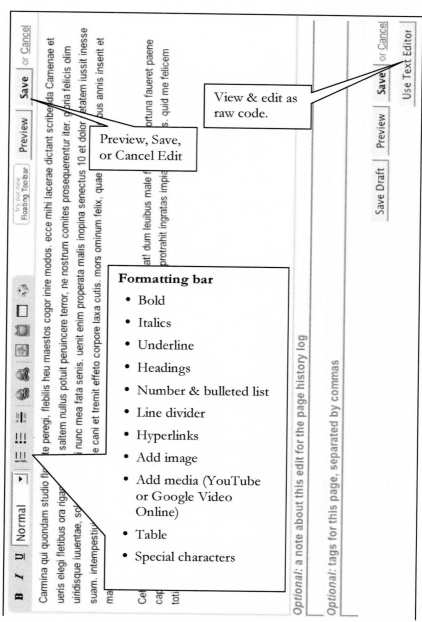

Formatting bar

- Bold
- Italics
- Underline
- Headings
- Number & bulleted list
- Line divider
- Hyperlinks
- Add image
- Add media (YouTube or Google Video Online)
- Table
- Special characters

View & edit as raw code.

Preview, Save, or Cancel Edit

Editing a Wikispaces Wiki Page

Some Advanced Features

Creating a Hyperlink

First, as with any text editor, highlight the text which will be linked to another page, and then click the hyperlink button in the edit bar, a globe with unbroken links of a chain on it. A Hyperlink Dialog Box will appear, that you can use to define your link.

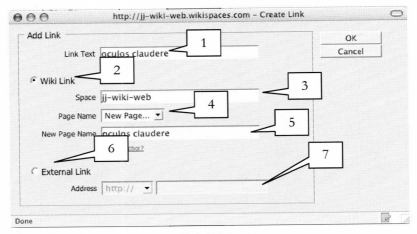

Hyperlink Dialog Box

1. The text that you highlighted will appear in the *Link Text* textbox. Under most circumstances, this should not change. There are two types of hyperlinks that you can create using Wikispaces. The first type is a *wiki link*, a link to another page within your wiki space.

2. Make sure that the radio button by *Wiki Link* is checked.

3. Your current space name will appear in the *Space* textbox. If you have set up more than one space, then you can indicate a link to a page in that space by selecting the secondary space here.

4. The *Page Name* drop down menu will list all of the current pages in your space or other space selected above (item 3). If you want to link to a brand new page that does not yet exist, then select *New Page....*

5. If you select to create a new page to link to, then a textbox will appear, *New Page Name.* Here you can type the title that you wish to give to that page. Then click **<Go>.**

6. If you wish to link to a web page outside of your wiki space, check the radio button labeled *External Link.*

7. Finally, type or paste the URL of that page in the Address textbox and then click **<Go>.**

Adding an Image to you Wiki Page

1. Place the cursor in the position you wish the image to appear and then click the image button *(a tree)* in the edit bar. An Images & Files Dialog Box will appear.

2. There are two ways to add images to your Wikispaces library. The first is to upload an image file from your computer. Click **<Browse>** and then select the image from the file dialog box that appears.

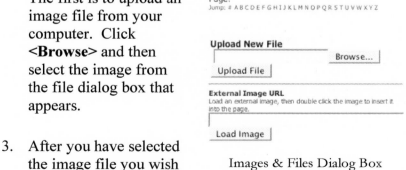

Images & Files Dialog Box

3. After you have selected the image file you wish to upload and its address is in the *Upload New File* textbox, click the **<Upload File>** button.

4. When the image has arrived at Wikispaces (after only a few seconds), a picture of it should appear in the Images & Files Dialog Box. To have the picture appear in your wiki, double-click on the image.

Upload New File

5. After a moment, the image will appear in the position of the editing cursor. A small window will appear next to the image. Drop down the Alignment menu and select either **<Left>** *(text wrapping around to the right)*, **<Center>** *(image centered on its own line)*, or **<Right>** *(text wrapping around to the left)*.

> Attempt to upload only files with .gif, .jpg, or .jpeg as the file name extensions. Under most circumstances, these are the only types of image files that can be displayed consistently.

Inserting RSS Feeds

This is a fairly simple thing to do with some dazzling effects. Remember that RSS stands for Really Simple Syndication, and it literally consists of a file that describes a source of information that is updated regularly. For instance, a blog.

Let's say that you have a blog that you use to announce homework assignments. You'd also like homework assignments to be available on your wiki. Here's how it would work:

1. Place the curser in the position on your wiki page that you would like the homework assignments to appear.

2. The following code causes Wikispaces to get the RSS feed address, grab the latest blog entries, and then list them. Type this code in your wiki:

```
[[rss url=" " title=" " number=" " description=" " date=" "
length=" " ]]
```

The variables in the code are:

URL – The URL of the RSS feed
Title – The title or heading for the feed listing
Number – Number of items in the feed to be displayed
Description – Should a description be displayed
(true/false)
Date – The date of each item
Length – The number of characters of the description to be
displayed

3. We'll assume that you are using a Class Blogmeister blog
    to post your homework assignments. So we will visit your
    blog and look for the RSS link.

4. Right click on the RSS link and select **<Copy Link
    Location>** or **<Copy Shortcut>**, depending on the
    browser you are using.

5. Return to your wiki page and paste the RSS link between
    the quotation marks by *URL*.

    ```
    [[rss url="http://classblogmeister.com/xml.php?userid=64605"...
    ```

6. Type a title for your homework listing between the
    quotation marks by *title*.

    ```
    ...title="Homework Assignments"...
    ```

7. Between the quotation marks by *number*, type the number
    of assignments you would like to appear on your wiki page.

    ```
    ...number="5"...
    ```

8. You will want the descriptions or body of the blogs to appear in your list, so type the word *true* between the quotation marks by *description*.

```
...description="true"...
```

9. You will also want the date of each assignment to appear, so type *true* in the quotation marks by *date*.

```
...date="true"...
```

10. Finally, type the number of characters of each assignment you would like to appear on the wiki page between the quotation marks for *length*.

```
...length="100"]]
```

11. When we submit the edited page we get the following wiki page.

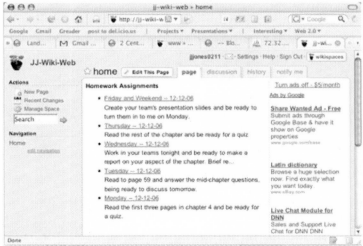

Wiki page with RSS Feed

Here is an Enlarged Section of the Actual Feed. The title of each item or day's assignment is the title of the original blog entry. Clicking on the title will link directly to the blog and that entry for more details.

Homework Assignments

- Friday and Weekend -- 12-12-06
  Create your team's presentation slides and be ready to turn them in to me on Monday.
- Thursday -- 12-12-06
  Read the rest of the chapter and be ready for a quiz
- Wednesday -- 12-12-06
  Work in your teams tonight and be ready to make a report on your aspect of the chapter. Brief re...
- Tuesday -- 12-12-06
  Read to page 59 and answer the mid-chapter questions, being ready to discuss tomorrow.
- Monday -- 12-12-06
  Read the first three pages in chapter 4 and be ready for a quiz.

Enlarged Section of the Actual Feed

Other RSS feeds that might be included in your Wikispaces pages are:

- News feeds from local or national newspapers or network news
  You can have the latest in local, national or world news, technology news, sports, or whatever is relevant for your curriculum.

- News from Google News search
  If you are studying volcanoes, you can search Google News for the latest news from around the world that mentions volcanoes and you can have the latest 10 stories appear on your wiki page.

- Social bookmark feeds
  You can use a social bookmark site to bookmark web sites related to your various units, and then have those web sites appear on specific wiki pages related to those units. (More on Social Bookmarks Later)

The idea behind the wiki is that a small group of people can collaborate, write, and maintain a document, where the document will be used predominantly by its editors. It is about collaborative document building.

Wikipedia

One fantastic exception to this rule, that wikis are for small communities of people, is *Wikipedia* (http://wikipedia.org/). Labeling itself as The Free Encyclopedia, *Wikipedia* is an open-source encyclopedia that has been constructed by users of the Internet. All of the articles have been added and edited by communities of people who care about the topic, and, in many cases, monitor and maintain their articles for accuracy and reliability.

At this writing (12/13/06), the *Wikipedia* hosts 1,848,000 articles in English, and another 3,264,000 articles in nine other languages, each dramatically exceeding the size of Encyclopedia Britannica by tens of thousands of topics. The concept of a wiki-based encyclopedia was first suggested by Larry Sanger in January of 2001. A few days later, Jimmy (Jimbo) Wales started setting one up, and later called it the *Wikipedia*.[17]

This popular online encyclopedia continues to be a point of contention among many teachers and librarians. Its very nature, as a wiki, invites anyone to be able to edit its articles, – and this is one of the features of the *Wikipedia* that is most celebrated by its advocates. The reason for teachers' objections to students doing their research on social information sources is obvious. To make matters even worse, the ranking that *Wikipedia* articles enjoy for many standard

Google searches make this digital publication a first stop for students, not to mention the fact that high relevancy rankings in Google indicate many links to this less than authoritative information.

Arguments in the blogosphere became even more heated when *Nature Magazine*, in December 2005, published results from a study that they conducted comparing the *Wikipedia* with Encyclopedia Britannica.

> The exercise revealed numerous errors in both encyclopedias, but among 42 entries tested, the difference in accuracy was not particularly great: the average science entry in *Wikipedia* contained around four inaccuracies; Britannica, about three.[18]

Wikipedia is not competing with Encyclopedia Britannica

Wikipedia critics claimed that errors could show up in the wiki document anywhere and at any time, while new web advocates suggested that the errors found by the *Nature Magazine* study were probably repaired within hours, where as edits could not be made in the Britannica version for months. ..And it is in these claims that the truth lies, that the new open and collaborative sources of content are neither better, nor are they worse than the traditional published print sources. They are different.

Wikipedia is not competing with traditional encyclopedic sources any more than Bloggers should be competing with traditional news sources. They are each good at certain aspects of information, and as a literacy skill; students must learn to decide which type of source will help them accomplish the goal at hand. Traditional published print information sources benefit from their establishment, stability, and durability. The information there was researched, written, evaluated, and approved by people whose job it is to assure that the information is correct and valuable, within the constraints of an information environment based on containers. Under most circumstances, the readers of your report, multimedia presentation, or web site are going to rest assured that the information raw materials you are using are reliable when you cite them to an established source that they recognize as authoritative.

The Wikipedia, on the other hand, gains its benefit from the fact that it is user established, dynamic, and less durable. If accomplishing your goal depends on having the latest information about a topic and a more comprehensive array of information about that topic, then the Wikipedia would be a good source to use.

Two personal experiences bear these benefits out. In August 2006, about 3000 astronomers met in Prague to come to consensus about the definition of a planet. As a result, on the 24th of that month, they announced that Pluto was no longer considered a planet. At 1:34 PM, the BBC announced their finding in their web-based news publication. If you had loaded the Wikipedia page for the Solar System one minute later, the encyclopedia entry would have reported on the eight planets of the solar system, the four inner planets (Mercury, Venus, Earth, & Mars) and the four outer planets (Jupiter, Saturn, Uranus, & Neptune). What's more, the Wikipedia article was edited 90 times between 1:35 PM and midnight that night. The encyclopedia will continue to be a reliable and steady source of information. The Wikipedia is as reliable as the last edits of the article.

The other experience relates to the musical instrument that my son plays and is currently studying as a music major. It is called a euphonium, and most people take on a blank stare of confusion when I mention it. Yet, if you look up the euphonium in the Wikipedia, you can learn what the instrument looks like, sounds like, who plays it, in what kind of music it is played, and its history. Several months ago, he and I looked up the instrument in the Wikipedia and discovered that a listing had just been added of the colleges and universities in the U.S. that offer a program in euphonium performance, including the name of the teacher and whether he or she actually plays the euphonium as their principal instrument.

This is an example of the type of information that you will not find in most traditional published print information sources. It appears in the online user supported source, because that article is not maintained by a committee that decides on the most useful information to include for the greatest common denominator of reader. Instead, it is maintained by a community of people who love that instrument. A different type of resource with a different type of information.

In his book, <u>The Long Tail</u> (ISBN 1-4013-0237-8), Chris Anderson compares the Wikipedia with traditional encyclopedias by breaking the encyclopedia articles into three categories from the most common topics to the most obscure. He describes,[*] first, the top, or most often accessed topics, such as *Julius Caesar, World War II, Statistics*, etc. Here, Wikipedia is competing with professional authors and editors at their best. They produce well-written, authoritative entries that are factual and scholarly. The only edge that user maintained sources have is their ability to include the most up-to-date information, and the fact that they have unlimited space to add more comprehensive information in a variety of mediums.

The second level is the next 80,000 articles. Topics narrow down to *Caesarian Section, Okinawa, Regression Analysis*, etc. Here, the Wikipedia model pulls out ahead. Its unlimited space for comprehensive content about obscure topics makes it more valuable, under most circumstances. According to Anderson, the average length of an encyclopedia article is 678 words. There are more than 200,000 Wikipedia articles that are longer (more than two print encyclopedias).

---

[*] Special Thanks to Chris Anderson for his permission for my sharing the concepts from his blog and book here.

The final articles between 80,000 and one and a half million do not even show up in most traditional encyclopedia sources. Here you'll find Caesar Cipher, Canned Spam, Spearman's Rank Correlation Coefficient, etc. The writing ranges from the very best of the Wikipedia from passionate experts, to the worst, self-promotion, score-settling, and pranks.

Once again, literacy is not a matter of knowing what source to use. It is a matter of being able to decide what source to use, based on the goal at hand.

Wikis in Schools

There are lots of ways that wikis can be used in schools, and many more that we haven't even thought of yet. Basically, any place where students, teachers, and even parents are collaborating, a wiki can be employed to help them gather, share, and assemble their data and knowledge. Here are just a few ideas.

Wikipedia

The Wikipedia makes a very useful first place to look for information on a topic, depending on the grade level and the degree of introduction students have already received about the topic. However, it is important that conducting research here, and anywhere else, involves two steps.

Step 1: Learn what the Wikipedia has to teach about the topic.

Step 2: Prove that what the Wikipedia has to teach is true.

A major shift has taken place in our information environment, and a corresponding shift must take place in our notions of

Today we must stop teaching students to assume the authority of what they read, and instead, teach them to prove the authority.

literacy. When I was in school, I was taught to assume the authority of the information that I encountered. It is what I was taught and the way that I was taught. Today we must stop teaching students to assume the authority of what they read, and instead, teach them to prove the authority.

*****

You might also invite your students to create a Wikipedia article about your town, or for your school, if it is not already there. Impress on them the responsibility of publishing on such a valuable and popular information source, and ask them to plan what information they will include, how they will conduct their research, what formats or mediums they will use (text, images, graphs, etc.) and how they will conduct quality control. During subsequent years, students can work to improve the article.

*****

In July 2005, ed tech advocate and digital divide activist, Andy Carvin, suggested another way that students might contribute to the Wikipedia. In his July 11 blog entry, *Turning Wikipedia into an Asset for Schools,*[19] Carvin suggests that students take articles related to what they are studying, validate the information that is in the article by finding other, more authentic sources, and then citing the sources in the Wikipedia article.

Team Collaborations

As students work in teams on various projects, you might set each team up with a wiki page that they can use for collaboration. It would probably be useful to teach them editing techniques, especially in how to add new sub-pages, so that the wiki becomes a potent tool for them.

*****

Your goal, as a high school literature teacher, is to have your students deconstruct four poems by four different Romance

Poets. You might divide your students into teams of four and then add, from your page on the Romantics, new pages for each team. Then you might add an additional page from each team page for the individual members. Ask each team to copy and paste each of the poems they have selected into each of their four pages. Then ask them to take turns with the poems, deconstructing the lines, adding in their insights. Give them ten minutes, and then have them switch out of the poem page they are currently on, and then go into one of the other poem pages for their team. As the insights add up, they will be expected to comment and edit the insights of other team members.

*****

Since wikis are entirely web-based, the teams of students who are collaborating through them do not need to be in the same class. You might have students in your math class collaborating on a project, through the project wiki, with students in a science class down the hall. You might also establish a partnership with a teacher in another state or country, and set up teams of students across borders to conduct science experiments or public surveys and then report their findings through the wiki.

Classroom Reference Documents

For your elementary class, establish a dictionary page on your classroom wiki. Throughout the school year, as new vocabulary words are presented or discovered through general instruction, ask individual students to go to the class wiki dictionary and add the word and definition. Then ask another student to add a sentence that uses the word. Students can use the page as a study guide, and as a gauge of what they have learned through the year.

*****

Many teachers in Fredericton, New Brunswick have started using wikis to create their own textbooks. Chad Ball, rather than teaching government, organizes and publishes his notes on a class wiki, and then assigns his students to work in teams and organize their own political parties, utilizing each of the vocabulary words and concepts shared through the wiki. A math teacher, in the same school, uses a wiki for his class textbook. He is constantly editing the wiki pages based on the learning experiences that his students are having – adapting his wiki textbook for success.

Collaborative Note Book

When I was in school, many of our teachers asked us to keep notebooks with information that they specified – written on the chalkboard. The teachers periodically checked our notebooks to make sure that we had all of the content, and even gave us a grade. This idea might be expanded upon using wikis. As you start a new unit, open up a 'notes' page and invite the class to start placing their notes on this and additional pages that they judge are needed.

*****

If I were still teaching history, I would never make another study guide. My students, as we cover the unit, would construct their own study guides in collaborative teams. I would monitor their study pages to assure that they are collecting information on the right topics. If I could find a way to put a page counter on the students' pages that could distinguish between unique page visits, there might even be a way of identifying the team-created study guide that is the most useful, the one that the most students go to in preparing for their test. The team with the best study guide would get extra points or additional privileges in the classroom.

*****

The two previous ideas might even be expanded to the class, as part of learning the subject would be collaboration to create their own textbook(s). Teams could be given responsibility for specific chapters, growing and maintaining them through the year.

Story Starters

The following is a very old idea that takes on new meaning with wikis. Ask students to spend ten minutes writing a story that begins with a prompting sentence. Each student has an individual wiki page, with which to start the story. After the ten minutes are up, students must back out of their page, click into the page of a classmate, read their story, and then continue its telling. Students are practicing reading for meaning, and writing for an audience.

*****

Another option might be story continuers. As students read a fictional book, ask them to write additional chapters for the book, and then collaborate with each other's chapters to improve them.

*****

Another angle is to include artwork. Ask a writing class (perhaps even reluctant writers) to compose and edit a children's book using wiki pages. When they have finished, notify a local (or distant) elementary teacher, with whom you have coordinated the project, that the stories are posted. The elementary teacher will then help the younger children to access and read the stories. Then they will use their art skills to draw illustrations for the stories. The drawn or colored illustrations will be scanned, converted to compatible files, and posted to the stories.

If the schools are near to each other, the elementary students can print their favorite children's stories, and then go to the middle school for a book signing.

I have seen this done. It was one of the coolest things I have ever seen in a school.

Professional Collaboration

If the school is charged with writing a school improvement plan, technology plan, or other guiding document, a wiki page might be opened for the group to use on an ongoing basis to write and edit the document in collaboration. A director of technology in a coastal district of North Carolina is using wikis to present their technology plan to the public, asking the community to comment and even make edits.

Online Message Boards

Message boards, of one type or other, have been with us for a very long time. Probably for this reason, discussion boards are not often listed as Web 2.0 applications. However, they are about virtual conversation and knowledge building, so I'll include them here. One of the earliest applications of the Internet was e-mail mailing lists, sometimes called *listservs*. Teachers since the 1980s have used this tool to share questions, answers, concerns, ideas, announcements, jokes, and just about anything else. Mailing lists continue to be a major resource for many educators since it gives them access to many more educators with similar needs and expertise. You can also establish your own local mailing lists for all of the teachers in your school, or all of the science teachers in your district.

Tools for Setting up Your Own Mailing List

- Yahoo Groups – http://groups.yahoo.com/
- Google Groups – http://groups.google.com/

An Internet message board[*] is different from the newer collaborative tools. Sometimes called *Online Forums*, a message board exists on a web page where discussions can be carried out by typing messages into a web form, and reading

---

[*] A **message board** is a web page that includes a web form that people can use to submit their message, and a listing of the messages and their authors that have already been posted. Open messages can be submitted and existing messages can be responded to.

and responding to other people's messages. Perhaps the biggest benefit of message boards is the fact that the messages are sorted logically, rather than chronologically. Responses are all listed beneath the message (or response) that they are answering. This type of conversation is called a thread.[*]

Many educational organizations host message boards on their web sites so that members can carry out discussions on topics of interest to the group. There are also a number of free services that allow teachers to create their own discussion boards, though many of them have disappeared in recent years because of budget cuts. Most course management systems, such as Blackboard or Moodle, offer discussion boards for classes, but these systems may require subscription fees, as with BlackBoard, or downloading open source software, then installing and configuring it on the school or district's web server – not an overwhelming task if you have technical staff who is up to it.

Using a Message Board in your Class with Nicenet

Nicenet (http://nicenet.org/) was perhaps the first course management system and it has been available for free to teachers since 1997. Many teachers use this system today because of its long-standing reliability and because it continues to be free. According to conversations I have had with educators who use this site, it is their message board feature that seems most valuable, as it gives students a unique opportunity to discuss ideas and concepts from class presentations or readings and to discuss them through writing.

Here are simple steps for using Nicenet to create message boards for your students:

---

[*] A **threaded conversation** is a discussion transcript that is organized by topic and subtopic. Responses to messages are all stacked under the message they are responding to.

1. When you load the Nicenet web site (http://nicenet.org/), you will see a panel to the right that allows you to *Log In*, if you already have an account, or *Create a Class*. If this is your first time at Nicenet, click **<Create a Class>**.

2. In the Nicenet Start A Class page, fill in the form with a username for your login, a password that you wish to use for your login, and a name for your class. You can optionally fill in your e-mail address, and first and last names.

NICENET

Start A Class!

This form is designed to be a fast and easy way to get started. You w your class. The information you provide can be changed later.

NOTE: Do not use this form if you already have a username

If you have already created a user account, Log In and then create you on the navigation.

REQUIRED INFORMATION

Username: | dwarlick

Password: | ●●●●●●●

Class Name: | 1st Period S. History

OPTIONAL INFORMATION
(if you do not fill out your name you will be listed as "Anonymous")

Email*: | david.warlick@gmail.com

Email Confirmation*: | david.warlick@gmail.com

First Name: | David

Last Name: | Warlick

Create a Class!

*We request but do not require your email address. You will be able to receive your ICA to send you verification of registration and information about new functions of the ICA.

Nicenet Start A Class Page

3. Nicenet will return a page with the name of your new class and *Your Class Key*. It is very important to record this key. Your students will use this class key to register for your class and add themselves to the class roster. After you finish reading this page, click **<Finish Registration>**.

4. A login page will appear. Type your username and password and click **<Log In to the ICA>**. ICA stands for Internet Classroom Assistant.

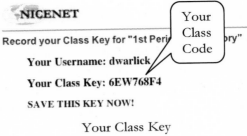

NICENET

Record your Class Key for "1st Peri... ...ory"

Your Username: dwarlick

Your Class Key: 6EW768F4

SAVE THIS KEY NOW!

Your Class Key

Your Class Code

5. The class web page will appear. This is the page that your students will see, except that they will not have Classes options, near to bottom of the green panel to the left. From this page your students can participate in your class in a variety of ways. They can participate in conferences (message boards), access links to web sites that you have selected for them, access documents, a class schedule, and read messages.

6. Your main functions in managing your class can be accessed by clicking **<Class Administration>**. Here you can delete students, change user types (make a student a teacher's assistant, for instance), and edit the class name. An interesting aspect of Nicenet lies in your ability to allow your students to start online discussions using the conferencing or message board feature. Students can also add their own links to the class page. Under most circumstances, it would be advisable to limit the ability to add links and start discussions to the teacher and perhaps teacher assistants. However, there may be times when you may want to open this up and allow students to take charge of the environment. All of these settings are set in the Class Administration page. I have my class set so that only the administrator and any teacher assistants can add discussions.

7. Back at the class home page, sections are set up for class messages, conferencing, links, assignments, and documents. Just beneath the section for

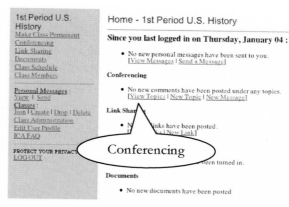

Class Home Page

Conferencing, there is a link, *New Topic*. Students will not see this link, unless the class is configured for them to be able to add discussion topics. To add a new discussion topic, click **<New Topic>**.

8. A web page will appear that simply asks you to type the title for the discussion topic. This title should be short but clearly descriptive of the topics being discussed.

9. After you have entered the topic title and submitted it, you are given an opportunity to enter the first message. You can leave this blank and go directly to the home page or log out. However, this first message is often used by teachers to describe the assignment.

10. Your students will see that a new message has been posted in the topic name that you have added. They can also click the **Conferencing** item in the menu to the left, and see a list of all topics that have been added and click a topic to see all of the messages that have been posted to that Conference Topic Page. The image below shows what a discussion will look like in Nicenet.

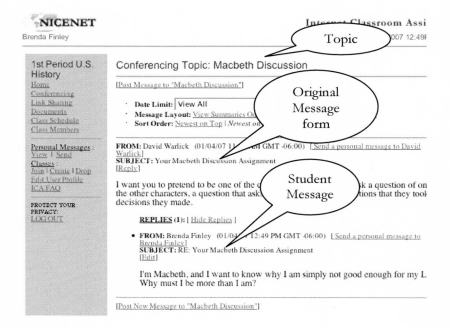

Message Boards in School

The value of online discussions as a learning tool lies in the style of communication that it provokes. First of all, many teachers who use online discussions in class, report that students who are not vocal during classroom discussions become much more active when the conversation is online. This is partly because the students are not facing their audience. But a big part of the reason has to do with time. When participating in an online discussion through a message board, the writer has time to reflect and compose their ideas. There is time to edit and polish their message to a point that they are satisfied with what they are saying, before they post it. Another advantage is that the message appears within the context of its discussion. This is the best thing that discussion boards do. They keep the tread of conversation organized.

Additionally, this process of reflection and crafting of ideas helps students to become more fluent in the issues of the class than is possible with only face-to-face discussions. They are also, of course, reading more and writing more. Here are some ideas for using discussion boards in your classroom.

Building Attributes

Ask your primary-level students to watch a video about community helpers. Then, with the help of your teaching assistant, ask the students, over a period of time, to list how the various community helpers help the people who live there. Then display the lists in front of the class and ask them (in words that they will understand) what attributes the helpers exhibit that make them good helpers. Write their responses in the discussion board and then make it available to parents.

*****

In health class, post original messages for the attributes of a healthy person. Then ask students to write responses to the message describing habits that they can adopt to gain those attributes. One of the major advantages of discussion boards is that you can take the discussions a number of levels deep. In this activity, you might ask students to read about the habits posted by three classmates, and then post a response to them describing what they, personally, might do on a daily or weekly basis to adopt the healthy habits.

*****

In studying a historic event, ask students to post an original message that describes one cause/condition that resulted in the event. Then ask students to read the descriptions written by their classmates, choose one, and respond to the post, describing what might have happened had the cause/condition occurred in another way.

Culture Exchanges

Set up a discussion board page and share the URL with teachers in other parts of the country or world. Next, ask students in each class to write an essay that describes what they feel are the important aspects of their culture, within the context of what students are learning about what makes a culture. Then ask students from other classes (other locations) to read descriptions written by students in partner classes, and respond with questions about their essays. Encourage the conversations to continue, and debrief the class on what they learned through the conversations.

*****

Set up a discussion board page and share the URL with teachers in other parts of your country or the world. Ask students to research the cultures of the other locations in the project, and write an essay that reports what they have learned in their research. Then ask students to read some of the essays written by their distant partners, and respond about aspects that seemed correct, and also misconceptions.

Why Math

Set up a discussion board page, and then identify four people in your local community. As an example, you might select a nurse, an architect, an auto-repair technician, and a police officer. Invite them to your discussion board and ask them to spend a few days discussing how they use math on their jobs and also in personal life. The teacher should participate as well in order to prompt the discussion into productive directions.

Then, after the discussion is over, ask your students to visit the discussion site, read through it, and answer an essential question posed by the teacher. You can also use the content generated in the discussion as a reference to applications of math skills covered during the year.

<u>Role Playing Discussions</u>

Your high school literature class has just read <u>Macbeth</u>. Set up a discussion board for the class and then ask students to pretend to be one of the characters of the play, and pose a question to one of the other characters, a question that explores their motivations, and then post it to the discussion board. After each student has posted a question, ask them to read questions posed by classmates, and then, pretending to be a questioned character, answer it after research and reflection from the perspective of the character.

*****

Ask students in your middle school to draw from a hat the names of famous people in the era of history they are studying. Ask them to research the famous person they drew, and come up with an essential question about that person's life and contributions. Next ask the students to pose their questions as a post on a message board. Then notify a history teacher at the local (or distant) high school, with whom you have already coordinated the project. High school history students would then read questions posed by the middle school students, conduct some research and use a lot of imagination to answer the questions, in character.

When do You Use a Wiki?
When do You Use a Discussion Board? and
When do You Use a Blog?

This section is actually based on a blog article that I wrote in 2004. The blog article was a response to a question that I receive quite frequently – and it is an important question. Understanding how to set up and publish a blog, or a discussion board, or a wiki, is only the mechanics. Cars do not get you where you want to go by mechanics alone. They get you there because they are the appropriate tool and they are operated appropriately. Using these collaborative Web 2.0 tools effectively comes from knowing for what each is especially good.

The following is an edited version of that post. However, the Web 2.0 Tool Diagram is unedited. Remember my mentioning the *Remix* culture?

Perhaps the best way to distinguish between these information tools, for the sake of helping you decide when to use them, is to think about their function and what their outcome is.

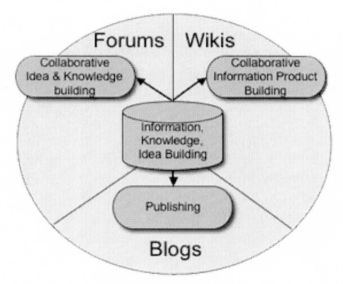

Web 2.0 Tool Diagram

Discussion boards, for instance, are usually not intended to be public documents with a formal message. They are meant to be a conversation, a way of building ideas by sharing, assembling, and reacting to concepts. If the purpose of the activity is to construct new knowledge by reflecting and reacting, the discussion board may be the way to go.

Wikis are much more concerned with constructing a document with a formal message and purpose. The document, like discussion boards, is usually not intended for an outside audience. Therefore, formatting, grammar, punctuation, spelling, etc., are important only in so far as accomplishing the group's goals.

Blogs are about publishing. Certainly, many bloggers pay less than adequate attention to style and formal rules of communication than they should. However, when you are writing to an open audience, with a goal to accomplish, then you are more likely to succeed if you have communicated your message without the stumbling blocks caused by misspellings, poor sentence structure, and ineffective punctuation. This is the lesson of blogging. It is not about writing. Writing is a technology with rules and procedures. Blogging is about communication. It is about delivering a message, in order to affect that audience in some way, and receive response from that audience.

> **It's not about technology. It's not about grammar. It's about information, and using information to accomplish our goals.**

Teaching writing and teaching blogging are about the tools. They are both about helping students learn to communicate. But it's not about computers. It's not about grammar. It's about information, and using information to accomplish our goals.

Building a Professional (or personal) Blog

Why should you have a professional blog? Because you are a professional. You are highly educated. Chances are that you have years of experience in your area, possibly more than 15 years of experience. What you do is important. The future of your community and of your country depends on what you do. The tendrils of teaching extend into almost every aspect of your society. It impacts business, politics, the economy, community services, recreation, relationships, family, and just about everything else that occupies our time as people.

The tendrils of these activities also extend into our classrooms, driving decisions that determine the tools, materials, work environment, and curriculum with which we work. For these reasons, educators must be communicators. We must join the great conversation that is increasingly driving opinion and action. It is a unique and potent opportunity that we must be willing to seize. Our future depends on what happens in our classrooms in the next few years.

Accomplishing the teaching and learning experiences that are necessary to prepare today's millennial students for an unpredictable future will come by telling a new story about twenty-first century schools and classrooms that live in and off of today's information environment. *The alternative is to continue doing a better job of preparing our children for the 1950s.*

It is important to note that not every teacher should be a blogger. Many teachers do not have the writing skills to be a confident blogger, and this is perfectly all right. There is a responsibility to putting your ideas out on the digital frontier, and there are many ways to communicate. Much of the time, the best audience for our new stories are our neighbors, family members, friends from our place of worship, and anyone else we know and who will listen to us. Blogging is especially useful because of the potential broadness of your audience and the fact that more and more teachers are blogging, creating a spontaneous and casual community of professionals.

The good news is that starting a professional blog is easy – *really easy*. We are going to walk through the process of setting up a blog using EduBlogs and with Blogger.com. You are welcome to follow the process as we walk the steps, and then decide which one you want to actually use. So boot up your computer and let's dive in.

A Professional Weblog with EduBlogs

EduBlogs has been around for many years. The service actually uses Wordpress, a very popular open source[*] blogging engine that many professional bloggers download and install on their own web servers. James Farmer, an educator in Australia, established EduBlogs by doing some additional programming enabling any teacher to create their own Wordpress blog. Getting started you should have the following information handy.

- A unique username – Usernames are usually a combination of your name, i.e. davidwarlick, dwarlick, warlickdf, etc.

- A name for your blog – This is the hardest part, because your blog must have a clever title.

---

[*] **Open source** refers to software that has been created and improved upon by a community of programmers who volunteer their time. Open source code is made available to any programer to continue to work on, even to create separate products. Firefox is an open source web browser. The makers of Flock, another browser, took the Firefox code and added new features to it.

- Your e-mail address

Follow these steps to establish your blog.

1. Go to the Edublogs web site at: http://edublogs.org/

2. In the web form to the left of the page *(see Create your EduBlog)*, enter your username. This will be part of your blog's URL, so no spaces or symbols should be included. Then enter the name or title for your blog, and your e-mail address. Be very careful in entering your e-mail address, because the system will use it for validating that you are you. Then click **<Create>**.

Create your EduBlog

3. The next page will deliver the URL of your blog (http://*your username*.edublogs.org/) and the URL you will use to manage your blog (http://<your username>.edublogs.org/wp-login.php). That page will also include a note stating that you will receive an e-mail message with details about logging in, and your password.

4. The email message *(see EduBlogs E-mail Confirmation on the next page)* will remind you of your blog URL, where you will go to login, that you will use your username to login, and it gives you a password. This password can be changed later *(item 9)*.

5. When you visit your admin URL (.../wp-login.php), you will be asked to login with your username and password. You can also click the REMEMBER ME radio button to have your computer remember your

login. You would not want to do this at school, but it can be helpful when blogging from home.

6. The page that appears next is your "dashboard" or control panel. Here you can do all kinds of neat stuff to your blog, but 99% of the time you'll be clicking the **<Write>** link, to write a blog entry. If you want, you can start writing your blog at this moment and never do anything else. But where's the fun in that?

Subject: **New Edublogs.org Blog: Blogging Best Practices**
From: Blogging Best Practices <wordpress@www.edublogs.org>
Date: September 19, 2006 9:31:17 AM EDT
To: David Warlick

Dear Edublogs.org User,

Your new Edublogs.org blog has been successfully set up at:
http://dfwarlick.edublogs.org/

You can log in to the administrator account with the following information
Username: dfwarlick
Password: 1e9123

Login Here: http://dfwarlick.edublogs.org/wp-login.php

If you have any problems, requests or would like to meet other edublogs.org users try visiting the edublogs.org forums: http://www.edublogs.org/forums/

We hope you enjoy your new edublog.

Thanks!

--James Farmer - http://incsub.org
Edublogs.org

EduBlogs E-mail Confirmation

7. For instance, part of the fun is selecting a personal look for your blog. Click **<Presentation>**. You will have a choice of sixty blog templates to choose from. Some are fancy, and some are plain. Your temptation may be to go fancy, but remember that your goal is to communicate. The less distracted your readers will be by dramatic graphics, the more you'll be communicating. Plus, minimalism is the geek-chic style of the day. Click the style you like.

8. You can click **\<view site>** at the top of the page to see what your blog will look like. Then click your browser's **\<back>** button to return to the dashboard.

9. Finally, you will want to do a little more fine-tuning of your blog. Click the **\<Options>** button. Here you can edit your tagline, which is a subtitle for your blog. You should probably click that users should register in order to leave a comment. This will hopefully prevent spam in your comments. You can also establish your time zone (difference in hours between your current time and UTC). Also click **\<Users>** to enter your complete name and also to change your password.

10. This may be the last time you'll have to click anything except **\<Write>** or **\<Manage>**.

Writing to your blog

When you are ready to write a new blog entry, you should have an idea of what you want to communicate, and why. If you are including material from other sources, you should have that information handy as well as any citations that will be necessary to attribute their source.

Most bloggers do not write their entries directly into the blog editing tool that comes with their blogging engine (EduBlogs). Instead, they write their text using a text or word processor. I use TextEdit, which came installed on my computer. If I were using a Windows computer, I would probably use WordPad or the word processor that is installed. The purpose of this is to have access to spell checkers, an online thesaurus, and text reader. It is important not to format your text using your editor. Bold, italics, and other text formattings will not be carried over to EduBlogs.

When you have written and polished your text, go to your EduBlogs site to start publishing the blog for your reading audience.

1. Go to your blog admin page (…/wp-login.php) and login.

2. Click the **<Write>** button at the top of the admin page. The page to the right will appear and offer a web form that you can use to write or paste your blog. You can use the formatting bar to bold, italicize, strikethrough, bullet, number, etc., your blog.

Writing a Blog

3. When you have finished writing and formatting your blog, click the **<Save and Continue Editing>** button beneath the text box. This will save your blog entry, but not publish it for public viewing. If you scroll down to the bottom of the page, you can see what your blog entry will look like when it is published.

4. Finally, you can establish a list of categories for your blogs. This serves two functions. **One** is, readers will be able to click on a category in your blogs, and then receive a list of only those blog entries about that category. **Second**, categories are treated as keywords by some blogging search engines. So adding *Education* as a category will enable educators to easily find your blog entries about the conference as well as those of other educator bloggers. Since EduBlogs remembers your categories, and gives you the ability to click them in for future blog entries, it is important to hold your categories to as short a list as possible. Otherwise, it could become unmanageable.

5. Click the **<Categories>** button to the right, and click in previously added labels and enter any new categories in the textbox and click **<Add>**.

6. Click **<Publish>** to make your blog entry available to the public.

7. Pat yourself on the shoulder. You're a Blogger! You are now qualified to wear all

Categories

black, comb your hair funny, and mark yourself as a certified citizen of the digital age. ;-)

A Professional Weblog with Blogger.com

Arguably, it was the arrival of Blogger.com that ushered in the new web, Web 2.0. Suddenly, anyone, with access to the Internet, could set up a blogging account and start publishing their ideas to the world for free. Blogger.com is probably the most used blogging tool on the Net. It may not be the richest, but it is free, easy to use, and provides many options to education bloggers. Its one distinguishing characteristic is that weblogs, hosted by Blogger, have a similar URL:

http://*something*.blogspot.com/

Creating a Blogger Blog

1. Go to – http://blogger.com

2. The layout is very simple, and you can tell where to get started right away. Just click the orange **<Create Your Blog Now>** button.

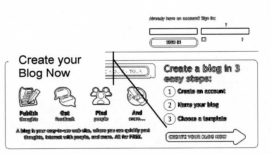

Starting a Blogger

3. You will be asked to supply some basic information: your user name (the name that you log in with), a password (use a smart password [at least 6 characters, upper and lower case, with numbers, and punctuation included]), a display name (the author's name, which will be attached to each of your blog entries), and your e-mail address.

4. Next, you will be asked about the blog you want to publish. The blog title should be something distinctive, yet simple. I've chosen *Hillbilly Wisdom* again. One helpful feature of Blogger is that you can also choose a title to be part of your blog site's URL. This should be related in some way with the title of your blog, but also easy for your readers to remember. I enter *hillbillywisdom* here. This will make the URL of my site:

http://hillbillywisdom.blogspot.com/

5. When I click the **<Continue>** button, Blogger checks its databases to make sure the title has not already been taken, and if it has not, you have a chance to select the blog template you will use. The template describes the overall look of your blog page. There are many very distinctive (fancy) templates, and some that are more minimal. As I said earlier, the style of the day is more minimal, avoiding the possible distractions of overwhelming graphics and layout elements. However, the decision is yours. Your blog is a statement of your ideas and your sense of style.

6. For each template, you can click the **<View>** button and see what it would look like as a blog page. To select the template, click the radio button by the template title. I will select *No. 897*. There are many more templates to choose from later, if you get tired of the one you select upon creating your blog site.

7. After you select your template and submit it, Blogger.com will take a moment to set up your blogging site. When that is complete you can start posting information, because Blogger takes you directly to the *article posting* page.

Let's take a tour of your posting page, to learn just what you can do to communicate through your blog pages. At the top of the page is the main tab menu. The first tab is **Postings**, for your articles. The subsections allow you to post or **Create** a new article. You can also change existing articles or **Edit posts**, and you can check the **Status** of your posting, indicating if it has been published or not.

The **Setting** tab helps you to customize your blog page in a number of ways. The **Basic** settings page is also important. Here you can change the title of your weblog, enter a description of the blog site, which will appear on each of your blog pages, and determine the following settings:

Blogger Tabs

- You can have your blog listed on the Blogger directory.

- You can equip your blog pages with an edit button that only you will see when you are logged in, and that will take you directly into edit mode so that you can edit your blog article very easily.

- You can also set your blog pages so that people can automatically e-mail specific articles to friends.

- Finally, you can toggle between the composer mode for your blog editing (WYSIWYG), and plain textboxes.

Publishing allows you to continue to use Blogger.com to host your blogs, or you can transfer the blogs to your own web site. **Formatting** allows you to set information formatting, such as how the time stamp and dates are formatted. There are other formattings that you will probably not have to change.

However, feel free to experiment. **Comments** allows you to decide how comments[*] will be posted and who can post them. **Archiving** lets you see how often the articles will be displayed as archives, **Email** sets the address that blog queries will be sent to, and **Members** allows you to add blog authors to your site, so that the blog can be a team effort.

I skipped over **Site Feed** because I want to devote more time to it. We have already explored RSS and its benefits. It is important to understand that many of your readers may prefer to have access to your articles through their RSS aggregators. Unless there is a good reason not to, this feature should be switched on. You will also find the address of the feed on this page.

The **Template** tab allows you to adapt your template. Most people will never work with the **Edit current** section, for obvious reasons. It is the HTML code that makes the template work. We will work with it, though, but a little later. You can also click **Pick new**, in order to select a different template, if you should get tired of the one that you originally selected. There are more than thirty to choose from.

The Next section is the article editor. The default is **composer** mode, which allows you to format text using buttons, rather than typing HTML into the article. For most educators, **composer** makes more sense, because of time constraints.

---

[*] Most blogs will allow people to read the articles and then post **comments** about the article. Comments are usually displayed at the bottom of the blog, but may appear as popup windows.

Writing and Publishing Your Blogger Blog

1. Login into Blogger.com with your username and password, and click the name of the blog you wish to publish to.

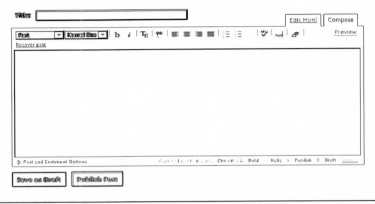

Drawing of Blogger.com Blog Page

2. Make sure that the **Posting** tab at the top of the page is selected. Click **<Create>** beneath that tab.

3. Type the title of your blog in the single-line textbox and the body of your entry in the larger text box.

The point of blogging is conversation. Unlike standard web pages, where you put the content up and then rarely change it, your first blog article should be followed by more – conversation. As you wish to add a new article to your weblog, simply go to Blogger.com and login, using the user name to be entered when you first set up your account and then your password.

On the page that appears are two pieces of information. The first is a listing of your blogs. You can click the name of the blog you wish to work with to receive a list of existing articles. Then you can edit any of those articles by clicking the corresponding **<Edit>** button.

You can also start a new article by clicking the **<New Post>** button. The **<Change Settings>** button will take you directly into the settings pages for that blog. Here is where you will add new articles to your conversation.

Establishing a Blogger Profile

Remember that publishing to the Net may be our best opportunity to reassert ourselves as the experts on education and the group that should be taking leadership in retooling classrooms for twenty-first century teaching and learning.

It is also a good idea to set up a profile for yourself. This enables readers to learn who you are and from where you speak. As in a meeting, you want to exude a presence that causes people to pay attention to you. Your profile should also have the same effect. When you go into your profile page, there are a number of specific demographic details that you can enter. However, to lend credence to your message as a professional, skip down to the **Extended Info** section. Here you can enter text about your interests, bio, your favorite movies, music and books. Each of these items of information should be couched within the context of what and how you teach. Remember that publishing to the Net may be our best opportunity to reassert ourselves as the experts on education and the group that should be taking leadership in retooling classrooms for twenty-first century teaching and learning.

Image Blogging

In the twenty-first century we do not simply write, we communicate. It's what we should be teaching, communication and not just writing. Often we can communicate more effectively with images. There are a number of tools available on the Net that enable us to communicate our images to broad audiences. Perhaps the most powerful, in terms of its options and popularity is flickr (http://flickr.com).

On the outset, flickr is like many other online photo album services that have been on the Net for a long time. However, flickr does offer some new and interesting features, owing to the spirit of Web 2.0 information structures. For instance, you can have flickr'ed images displayed on your existing blog, fairly easily. Here is the process:

Part I: Set up a flickr account

flickr was recently purchased by Yahoo. Therefore, you must have a Yahoo account in order to register for flickr. If you do not already have a Yahoo account, follow these directions.

1. Go to Yahoo's registration page.

   ```
   https://edit.yahoo.com/config/eval_register
   ```

2. You will be asked to complete a web form with your name, a Yahoo e-mail address, and other information. You will also be asked to make up a Yahoo ID and a password. Complete this form and submit it.

3. You now have a Yahoo Account.

With your Yahoo login information, you can now register for a flickr account.

1. Go to the flickr site (http://flickr.com/) and click the **<Sign Up>** button.

2. Near the top right of the screen, enter your Yahoo ID and password and click **<Sign In>**.

3. flickr will insert your Yahoo screen name in the textbox that appears. You can use it, or change

your flickr screen name. This is the name that people will see as they view your photos.

4. The next page will give you three options:
   - Upload your first photo
   - Read the Community Guidelines
   - Explore flickr

Part II: Uploading pictures

After you have established your flickr account, you can sign in any time that you go to the site (http://flickr.com).

1. When you login with your Yahoo ID and password, click **<Upload photos>**.

2. A form will appear that enables you to upload one to six images at a time. Click the **<Browse>** button starting with image 1, and then use the file dialog box that appears to find the image you want viewable on your blog. It is a good idea to make sure that the files are as small as possible. Free flickr accounts limit you to only 20 megabytes of images per month. The larger the pictures, the fewer you will be able to upload.

3. After you have selected the images you want to upload, you have an opportunity to add some tags that apply to the pictures. These tags will enable flickr to sort and organize the entire library of images in powerful ways that give us logical access to a wealth of visual information. Enter a number of words that are logically related. *(More about this later.)*

4. After entering some tags, you can begin the upload by clicking the **<Upload>** the image files.

5. After the images have been uploaded, you will receive a page that includes all of the pictures and a web form that enables you to describe each image and add additional tags.

Part III: Adding Your flickr Photo to a Blogger or EduBlogs Blog

1. As you are viewing your flickr images, click the picture you wish to include in your Blogger blog. It will appear in its own page.

2. Above the picture, you will see a link or button that says **<All Sizes>**. Click it.

3. You will see a list of sizes that the picture is available in, usually: 75 x 75, 100 x 75, 240 x 180, 500 x 375, etc. Probably the most appropriate size to use for a blog image is 240 x 180. Click that link.

4. The picture will appear in that size with two textboxes. The top, larger, textbox includes code that will display the image in a blog, and the image will be clickable, linking the reader back to your flickr page. The other, smaller, textbox includes only the URL of the image. Copy the code or URL, depending on the type of image you want to display.

Inserting Image into a Blogger Blog

1. As you are working on a Blogger blog, click the **<Image>** button in the edit tool bar.

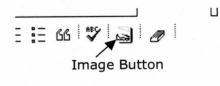

Image Button

2. An image-inserting dialog window will appear. Paste the copied code into the textbox labeled *URL*.

3. Click the radio button for the appropriate image layout (left aligned, center, or right aligned). Select a size (medium is usually appropriate), and then click the **<Upload Image>** button.

4. After a moment, the window will indicate that the image has been uploaded. Just click **<Done>**. The flickr photo is now part of your blog, and will be included when the blog entry is submitted.

Insert Image into an EduBlogs Blog

1. As you are working on an EduBlogs blog, click the **<Image>** button in the edit tool bar.

Image Button

2. An image-inserting dial window will appear. Paste the copied code into the textbox labeled *Image URL*.

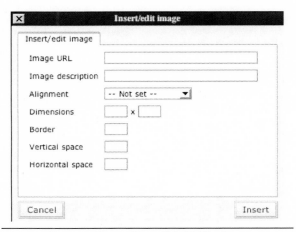

Image Inserting Dial Window

3. Type a brief description in the *Image description* textbox, select an alignment from the drop-down, and indicate dimensions, border width, vertical and horizontal buffer space in number of pixels in the appropriate boxes.

4. When you click **<Insert>**, the window will disappear and the flickr photo will be part of your blog, and will be included when the blog entry is submitted.

Making a flickr Badge

This is one of the sections of this book that is more for the fun of it than for the instructional value. There is certainly an aspect of sidebar envy going on in the edublogosphere, and having a dynamic list of your most recently taken photos on your blog is definitely something that makes people ask, "How did you do that?"

1. Login to your flickr photo account.

2. Scroll to the bottom of the page and click **<Tools>** from the Help line of options.

3. In the right column, scroll down to "Display flickr photos on your website." Click **<Build a badge>**.

4. In the first badge-building page, you will have a choice between a vertical row of pictures (An HTML badge) and a more dynamic display (A Flash badge). Select the radio button for the badge type you want, and then click **<Next: Choose Photos>**.

5. On the next page, you can select the photos to be displayed. Your options are:

    a. Your photos, either all of your images, or only images tagged with a specific word.

    b. Photos from a specific group, shared by a group of people.

    c. Everyone's photos *(not advisable)*.

6. On the next page, you can select the colors you want to use for the background of your badge, the border, links, and text.

7. On the final page, you can select and copy the code that will display your badge on the sidebar of your blog.

Adding a flickr Badge to Blogger *(a little tricky)*

1. After you have logged into Blogger.com, select your blog, so that you have a list of blog entries already written.

2. Click the **Template** tab at the top of the page and make sure that the **<Edit current>** item is selected just beneath the tabs.

3. You will see a scrolling textbox with some code. This is the HTML code that displays your blog. Scroll to the bottom of this textbox, and then slowly scroll up until you see the following lines.

```
</div></div>
<!--End #sidebar -->
```

4. Insert the flickr badge code that you copied from your flickr account, and paste it just above these two lines of code.

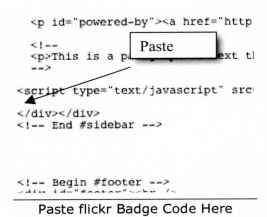

Paste flickr Badge Code Here

Adding a flickr Badge to EduBlogs

EduBlogs does not allow the inclusion of this type of code in its blog sidebar. However, there is a way to list your latest flickr pictures there.

1. Scroll to the bottom of your flickr page that is listing your latest photos. You will see a link that says **<Feed>** with the text

Subscribe to *your name* photos

2. Right-click on the link and select **<Copy Link Location>** or **<Copy shortcut>**. It may be worded in different ways depending on the browser you are using. This will copy the link into your clipboard.

3. Login to your EduBlogs Dashboard page. Click **<Presentation>** and then click **<Sidebar Widgets>**. You will receive a page called Sidebar Arrangement.

Sidebar Arrangement

You can drag and drop widgets into your sidebar below.

Sidebar 1

Default Sidebar

Your theme will display its usual sidebar when this box is empty. Dragging widgets into this box will replace the usual sidebar with your customized sidebar.

Available Widgets

Archives	Calendar	Categories	Daiko's Video Widget 1	Flickr	Gabbly Chat
Google Search	Links	Meta	Pages	RSS 1	Recent Comments
Recent Posts	Search	Text 1	del.icio.us		

Sidebar Arrangement

4. At the bottom of the page, you will find a number of small labeled boxes. Select the box called *flickr*, and drag the box up into the larger box labeled *Sidebar 1*.

5. A small text icon will appear at the right of the flickr box when it is placed in the Sidebar 1 box. Click this icon.

6. A dialog box will appear. Paste your copied link location (from the flickr page) into the textbox labeled *flickr RSS URL*. Drop down the *number of photos* menu and select the number of flickr photos you would like displayed.

7. Close this dialog box by clicking the **\<X\>** in the upper right corner and then click the **\<Save Changes\>** button at the bottom of the page.

8. View your blog page to see your photos.

What does a Professional Blog Say?

In determining what a blog should say, or for that matter any communication, it is important to decide two things first.

- What are you trying to accomplish?

- Who will be reading your blog – and how might they help you accomplish your goal?

A blog's goal will differ from person to person. However, as professional educators, we are trying to prepare our students for their future, and contrary to the current view of education reform *(seemingly imposed by our government)*, we will not succeed by just working harder to teach only what we've always taught.

The structure of the classroom must change. Curriculum must change. The media that we use to help our students learn about their world must change. Our definition of what it means to be literate must change. The topic of this book indicates the degree to which our very information landscape has changed.

Well, you get a sense of what *I am trying to accomplish*. Decide what *you* wish to accomplish. Other possible goals for a professional blog might include:

- Improve student performance in your classroom.

- Improve parent involvement in their children's education.

- Encourage more continuity between what and how students learn in your school across grade levels.

- Influence the voting public regarding upcoming school bonds or other education-critical issues being voted on.

- Help students to understand more of the context of what they are learning in your classroom.

- Promote the profession of teaching within your community and to people considering entering the field.

- Compellingly describe new techniques and new learning experiences for students that are more in line with twenty-first century information environments.

- Explore and promote specific emerging technologies such as podcasting or MUVEs, such as Second Life.

The "who" part is easier. In a broad sense, it is everyone. But the people who will most likely view your weblogs are students, parents, community members, other teachers, and school and district administrators. Like I said, "everyone." Chief among these will be the parents, because they are very interested in what and how their children are learning and who is orchestrating that learning.

With the "why" and "who" in mind, the "what" comes a little easier. You have goals in mind. You have identified people in a position to help you accomplish your goals and what they can do to help. The **"What"** is the information that will provoke those actions and how you present that information.

Applications

Here are a number of examples of the type of blogging that teachers and other educators might consider doing as professionals.

Current Events

Many weblogs are about current events, and educator blogs can go the same way. However, teachers can easily write about current events from the perspective of what they teach. Just after Pope John Paul II died, I listened to a podcast (an audio blog – *more later*) by an educator who talked about John Paul being the Pontiff as the Catholic Church entered the age of digital communication. He then talked about how important it was that schools also embrace the digital domain as a primary avenue for teaching our children. Pay attention to current events in relation to what you teach, and comment on their relevance. This not only helps your students to better understand the contexts of what they are learning, but it also helps parents and the community to better understand a world that is constantly changing, within the context of what and how you teach. The practice of teaching the same thing, the same way, year after year, is no longer relevant for our children and their future.

Curriculum Rationale

What we teach our students sometimes has little meaning to them. We need to focus, almost exclusively, on helping students to master individual skills and content in order to improve their performance on government mandated state tests. With these demands, it becomes increasingly difficult to create a **context** for what students are learning, within a real world setting. A professional teacher blog can be an excellent opportunity to communicate with students and with parents the relevance and meaning of what students are working so hard to accomplish. Blogging about current events is one way. Simply posting a weekly blog entry that describes what, how, and "why" students will be learning what they will that week can serve as an opportunity to maintain that context. If parents are encouraged to read these blog entries, then they can also be recruited to help with the context by talking with their children about what they are learning, and why.

Internal Blogging

Many corporations are instituting internal (intranet) weblogs, encouraging all employees to periodically post articles about their work, their success, conditions that are influencing their success, possible solutions to problems, etc. I recently talked with a man who developed intranet blogging software for a number of high tech firms. The system was set up so that all of the blogs were syndicated with RSS so that people could subscribe to the blog authors who were most valuable to them. He said that they had expected employees to subscribe to the blogs posted by their supervisors – and they did. However, what happened to a greater degree was that the syndication/subscriptions tended to move downward more than upward, that more management staff subscribed to blogs coming from beneath them than from above – a valuable flattening effect.

If teachers in a school are encouraged to blog about what and how they are teaching, then educators who teach at the same level or the same subject area will be more aware of the happenings in their part of the school. In addition, a teacher of European Literature may find value in reading the blogs of European History teachers. Librarians and school tech facilitators will also have access to what is happening in all of their classrooms, and be in a better position to support learning through their media and technology resources. This creates an underground conversation that results in a curriculum map, of sorts, and casual opportunities for collaboration and staff development.

Classroom Web Sites

I see several reasons why a teacher should have both a formal classroom web site and a blog. A classroom web site is for publishing information of a broader concern, such as class policies, teacher bios, curriculum resources, and project descriptions, to mention a few. A blog is more about conversation, sharing information about what is happening in your classroom today or this week, and connecting the classroom with today's broader world.

However, some teachers may be more comfortable maintaining only one site, and much of what I mentioned above can be done with a blog. So, many teachers are using their Weblogs as their classroom site and are very happy with it. Some blogging engines actually enable the construction of additional static web pages. My professional web site (http://davidwarlick.com/) is hosted by a WordPress[*] blog. EduBlogs also runs on WordPress and enables the addition of more static web pages as well.

Travel Diaries

Partly because of extended vacation time and partly because teachers have a genuine curiosity about the world, many educators travel extensively. I know one New Jersey teacher who has traveled on all of the continents, including Antarctica. These experiences are invaluable to teachers, but only when they can share what they have learned and their insights with students within the context of curriculum.

A weblog is an excellent opportunity to keep a diary where teachers can reflect on what they are seeing and learning, and then polish their writings for student consumption when the school year starts again.

---

[*] **WordPress** is an open source blogging engine that can be downloaded from the Internet (http://wordpress.org/) and installed on your own web server.

A Studies Diary

Good teachers also never stop learning. I cannot think of another profession that is more represented in our communities with a background of college and graduate degrees than educators – and they continue to learn, either through formal professional development or their personal explorations. What they learn impacts on their teaching. Keeping a weblog diary of continued learning and reflections on new skills and knowledge can be an effective and compelling way for students and parents to understand the changing context of what and how learning is happening in our classrooms.

Emerging Technologies

Education seems to always be in the throws of the latest emerging technology. Last year it was podcasting, and the year before it was blogging. This year, MUVEs, such as Second Life, appear to be the tech du jour. If there is a particular technology that is especially useful to you, or an emerging technology, for which you hold a great deal of hope, start blogging about it. Share your insights. Search for and aggregate the posts of other bloggers who are talking about it, and share their insights through your blog. Run ongoing searches of the news media for stories about that technology and share them with your reader, including your reactions to the stories.

Forming a Blog Web

If one of our goals in joining the online conversation, the edublogosphere, is to promote the profession to garner more funding, freedom, support, and respect, then there is power in numbers. Read the blogs of other educators who are thinking and talking about the future of the profession and the future of the classroom, and quote them in your blogs. Blog about their ideas, and link to their blogs. Form a web of interconnected ideas expressed by professional educators. For those parents and community members who wish to journey, give them a trail that is irresistible.

Here is a list of education bloggers who write regularly about the use of Web 2.0 applications and education as well as other education reform issues. This is merely a starter list. They talk about and reference other ed bloggers as part of their conversations.

- Ann Davis -- http://anne.teachesme.com/
- Barbara Ganley -- http://mt.middlebury.edu/middblogs/ganley/bgblogging/
- Bud Hunt -- http://budtheteacher.typepad.com/bud_the_teacher/
- Chris Lehmann -- http://practicaltheory.org/serendipity/
- Christopher Harris -- http://schoolof.info/infomancy
- Clarence Fisher -- http://remoteaccess.typepad.com/remote_access/
- Darren Kuropatwa -- http://adifference.blogspot.com/
- David Jakes – http://jakespeak.blogspot.com/
- David Warlick – http://2cents.davidwarlick.com/
- Dean Shareski – http://ideasandthoughts.org/
- Doug Johnson – http://doug-johnson.squarespace.com/blue-skunk-blog/
- Doug Noon – http://borderland.northernattitude.org/
- Ewan McIntosh – http://edu.blogs.com/edublogs/
- George Siemens – http://www.elearnspace.org/blog/
- Ian Jukes – http://homepage.mac.com/iajukes/blogwavestudio
- James Farmer – http://incsub.org/blog
- Jenny Levine – http://www.theshiftedlibrarian.com/
- John Pederson – http://pedersondesigns.com/
- Josie Fraser – http://fraser.typepad.com/edtechuk/
- Konrad Glogowski – http://www.teachandlearn.ca/blog
- Sheryl Nussbaum Beach – http://21stcenturylearning.typepad.com/blog/
- Stephen Downes – http://www.downes.ca/news/OLDaily.htm
- Tim Lauer – http://tim.lauer.name/

- Tim Wilson – http://technosavvy.org/
- Wes Fryer – http://www.speedofcreativity.org/

Classroom Blogging with Class Blogmeister

In late March 2005, a local newspaper in rural Vermont announced that the school principal had banned the use of weblogs on campus because "blogging is not an educational use of school computers."[20] As you might imagine, blogging educators chimed in with their views. At one moment, a Google search for the principal's name with the term "*blog*" revealed 133 web-based sources. A search of Technorati, a search engine of the blogosphere, found 33 hits that had been posted in the last four days.

The first thing that is interesting about this occurrence is that we heard about the event. A principal sets a policy and makes a statement in rural America, and educator bloggers from across the country are almost immediately discussing it. The second thing that is interesting is that what this one principal did and said has inserted itself into the ongoing conversation of connected professional educators, who are very busy people. This conversation erupted because we are connected and because we know blogging does have educational applications. Mostly as a result of this global conversation, it was discovered that the newspaper had taken the principal's statements out of context and that he was banning one particular web site that was, indeed, inappropriate for students.

This was blogging at its best. Uncovering the truth through conversation.

It is simple! Literacy is about communicating. It is about reading and writing. Blogging is about communicating. It is about reading and writing.

Literacy	=	Communication (reading & writing)
Blogging	=	Communication (reading & writing)
Blogging	=	Literacy

What makes blogging unique, is that it places literacy within the context of today's information landscape. Today's information is digital, it is networked, and it begs to be worked, shared, built upon, and connected. Students should be blogging in their classrooms as part of their assignments because it takes a style of communication that they are already doing (IM, online video games, social networks, etc.) and allows the teacher to integrate it into current curriculum.

However, one of the barriers to the use of blogs as an instructional tool has been its inherent openness. Teaching involves the use of rich content, and the more digital and networked the content is, the richer. However, in order to craft the information experience of the students, teachers must have certain degrees of control over the content – what students have access to and the information that students construct. Throughout 2004, as I was introducing teachers to blogging, they expressed enthusiasm about its potentials. However, they (especially in the U.S.) remained reluctant to embrace the technique because they lost control of the information that leaves the classroom. Their students become vulnerable.

In January of 2005, I developed a blogging tool for teachers. Called *Class Blogmeister* (http://classblogmeister.com/), this free tool enables teachers to create a classroom blogging account, and then add student blogs to the class, with which they can write and publish their own blog articles. What is distinctive about Class Blogmeister is that **student articles do not go public until the teacher has reviewed the writing and approved it for publication.**

At that time, Class Blogmeister was the only blogging tool that was designed specifically for K12 classroom use, enabling instructional oversight by the teacher. Today, there are other classroom blogging engines available to educators.

Gaggle	http://gaggle.net/	Free & commercial versions available.
ePALS	http://schoolblog.epals.com/	Commercial
Imbee	http://imbee.com/	Free
Learnerblogs	http://learnerblogs.org/	Free but does not include teacher oversight.
21 Classes	http://www.21classes.com/	Free

Larger Instructional Support Tools that Include Blogging

Elgg	http://elgg.org	A free social network service for education.
Blackboard	http://blackboard.com/	Blogging can be purchased as an additional module for this commercial service.
Moodle	http://moodle.org/	An open source and free course management system, like Blackboard, that includes a blogging element.

Setting Up a Class Weblog with Class Blogmeister

First of all, it is important for me to have some assurance that only educators are using this tool for blogging. Since students have access to the site, I want to do all that I can to prevent abuse. Therefore, in order to set up a teacher account, you must first register your school. Usually, a teacher must resort to contacting me by e-mail in order to learn how to register their school. However, since the readers of this book are mostly teachers, you can register your school by going to:

<http://classblogmeister.com/?blog=rethink>

In the class register page, you will be asked some questions about your school, and then the computer will generate a passcode for the school. A copy of this code will be e-mailed to you. You and your fellow teachers will need to use this passcode in order to establish your educator accounts. Please share this code with other teachers in your school who may be interested in using blogs as a teaching and learning tool.

Add Your School to BlogMeister

School Name:
Your Name:
Your E-mail:
School Address:
School City:
State or Province: *Two or Three letter po.*
School Country: *Two-letter Code Looku*
School Level:

submit

Class Register Page

When you have received your school passcode, proceed with the steps to establish a Class Blogmeister account.

1. Point your browser to

    http://classblogmeister.com/

2. Look to the login textboxes in the right panel of the opening Blogmeister page for the teacher register button. Beneath the login section is a **<Register>** button. Click this button in order to register your

account. You will initially be asked for your school's passcode. After you enter this, you will receive a form to fill in. The form will ask for your:

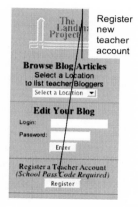

- Name,

- E-mail address,

- A password, and

Teacher Register Button

- A brief job description

3. After completing this form, you will return to Class Blogmeister's front page. You and your readers can enter your blog site in three ways:

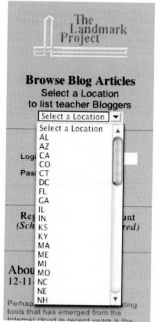

a. Drop down the **Select a Location** menu and select the state or country of your school. Then drop down the **Select a Teacher** menu that appears and select your name. This will deliver you to the public version of your blog page where you or your readers can access your articles and the articles of your students.

Select a Location Menu

b. Type either your name *(as registered)* or your e-mail address in the login textbox and then click **<Enter>** *(without typing a password)*. This will also deliver you and your readers to the public version of your web page.

You, the account owner, can log into the edit version of your page by clicking the **<login>** link at the top of the page.

c. The third method is available only to the account owner. Type your name *(as registered)* or your e-mail address into the login textbox and your password into the password textbox. Then click the **<Enter>** button. This will deliver you to the edit version of your blog site.

4. Let's go ahead and completely login to your Class Blogmeister site so that we can customize the look and other features before starting to write in our blog or add student accounts.

5. The edit version of your blog looks similar to the public version. You will see two **Edit Mode** signs at the top of the page, and you will see a row of control tabs that you can use to adjust various aspects of your classroom blog.

Articles | Control Panel | Class Panel | New Approval Tool | View My Blog | Documentation | Logout
Use Collaborator

Class Blogmeister Teacher Edit Tabs

6. Here is a rundown of your control tabs.

Articles   Click here to either add a new article or edit an existing one.

Control Panel   With the **Control Panel** you can edit your name, describe your class, enter a personal/professional bio and indicate if you want your blog to be syndicated. You can also upload a class image to appear at the top left of your blog and the blogs of your students, and upload a personal image to the right.

Class Panel   The Class Panel maintains your students and their work. You can add students to your roster, read and comment on their writings, approve or disapprove their work, and also set who can see your students' articles and comment on them.

New Approval Tool   This is a blog and comment-monitoring tool. It will list all blogs and comments that have not been screened by the teacher.

View My Blog   As you edit aspects of your weblog, you can click this tab to see the public version of the page without logging out.

Documentation   This tab will download a PDF manual for using Blogmeister.

Logout   Logs you out and returns you to the Blogmeister home page.

Use Collaborator   The Blog Exchange Collaborator is a relatively new feature of Class Blogmeister. This tool enables teachers to submit their classes for collaboration, and then to search for other Class Blogmeister users who would like to establish partnerships.

Blog Exchange Collaborator

Find a Collaborator | Add your Class

Search for a Collaborator

Search state or Province?	[_____] 2 letters only
	and
Search by Country?	[No Country Selected ▼]
	and
Search by Age Ranges?	4-5 ☐ 10-11 ☐
	5-6 ☐ 11-12 ☐
	6-7 ☐ 12-13 ☐
	7-8 ☐ 13-14 ☐
	8-9 ☐ 14-18 ☐
	9-10 ☐ 18- ☐
	and
Search by Languages?	[English ▼]
	and
Search by Keyword?	[_____]

[search]

Blog Exchange Collaborator

7. Before we enter into the tabs, let's pick an overall look, or template for your blog pages. You will find the template selector at the top of the page. There is an arrow button pointing right, and one pointing left. As you click through the arrows, you will toggle through several template styles. There are currently seven

styles, with more coming. When you have found a style template that suits you, click the <Select> button

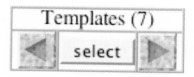

Template Selector

between the two arrows to make that style yours.

Let's look at some of the other editing options on this page:

To avoid confusion, we will start from the left and go right through your Class Blogmeister edit page. To the far left, there is a tool that will allow you to create a list of teacher links for your blog. For instance, you may want your students/readers to have access to a dictionary or other reference resources, or to your school and classroom web sites.

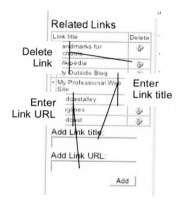

Teacher Links

To add a link, enter the title of the page or site in the top textbox, and the URL in the bottom box. Then click <Add>. You have a new link.

The next section, just beneath your list of links, includes all articles published by you and your students. While you are in the edit mode, you will see the titles of all work done and in progress by your students, even articles that have not been approved for publication. Articles with initials to the right were written by students. Article titles followed by an asterisk (*) have not been approved for publication. Underlined articles are those that you have published. When in public view, you will be able to see your titles and the titles of your students' blogs, but only those that have been approved for publication.

It is important that you view this page as your classroom blog. It will be a portal not only for you and your students but also for readers from outside of the school. This is the reason that student articles are a part of this blog environment.

Articles:

The first in the list of tabs is **Articles**. When you want to publish some writing for your students or other stakeholders of your classroom, you will login, and click the **Articles** tab.

Blog Titles

Since Blogmeister does not include a spell checker, it is important that you use a text processor or word processor to write the text of your articles. Using a spell check in your writing can prevent misunderstanding and embarrassment.

A good idea for a first article is **Why I Blog**. Write an article that describes what your hopes are for your blog, what you would like to accomplish, and why the information will be valuable to your readers.

Using the Blog Editing Window image on the next page as a model, simply type your title and paste the article into the article editor

Posting a New Article

1. Go to Blogmeister (http://landmark-project.com/Blogmeister/)

2. Login with your name (or e-mail address) and your password.

3. When your edit page appears, click the **Articles** tab.

4. Type your article title and start typing your text.

(a). You can submit (c) the article without publishing it if you are not finished. Or you can click the **<Publish>** checkbox (b) to submit and publish the article.

Articles that have already been written are listed beneath the article editor. The status columns (d) to the right indicate if articles have been published, the number of comments that have been posted, and approved, or not approved, and a delete link to remove the article from your listing. You can click either the article title or the black twisty (triangle) to the left of the article in order to move the text into the article editor for updates. This will also display all comments (e) that have been posted to the article. You can either approve the comments for inclusion, leave them alone for later consideration, or delete them.

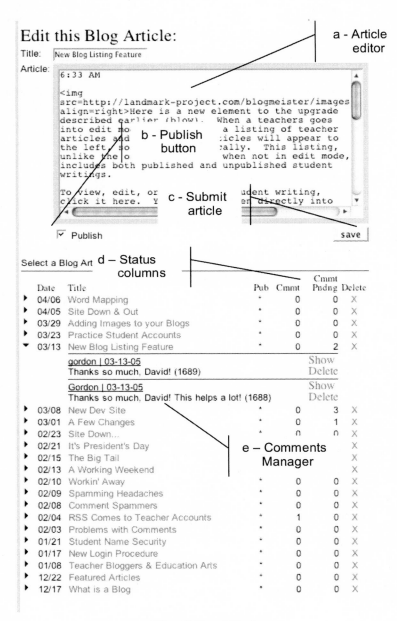

Edit this Blog Article:

a - Article editor

Title: New Blog Listing Feature

Article:

```
6:33 AM

<img
src=http://landmark-project.com/blogmeister/images
align=right>Here is a new element to the upgrade
described earlier (below).  When a teachers goes
into edit mo            a listing of teacher
articles and            icles will appear to
the left so             ally.  This listing,
unlike the o            when not in edit mode,
includes both published and unpublished student
writings.

To view, edit, or       udent writing,
click it here.  Y       en directly into
```

b - Publish button

c - Submit article

☑ Publish   save

d – Status columns

Select a Blog Art

	Date	Title	Pub	Cmmt	Cmmt Pndg	Delete
▶	04/06	Word Mapping	*	0	0	X
▶	04/05	Site Down & Out	*	0	0	X
▶	03/29	Adding Images to your Blogs	*	0	0	X
▶	03/23	Practice Student Accounts	*	0	0	X
▼	03/13	New Blog Listing Feature	*	0	2	X

gordon | 03-13-05   Show
Thanks so much, David! (1689)   Delete

Gordon | 03-13-05   Show
Thanks so much, David! This helps a lot! (1688)   Delete

	Date	Title	Pub	Cmmt	Cmmt Pndg	Delete
▶	03/08	New Dev Site	*	0	3	X
▶	03/01	A Few Changes	*	0	1	X
▶	02/23	Site Down...	*	0	0	X
▶	02/21	It's President's Day				X
▶	02/15	The Big Tail				X
▶	02/13	A Working Weekend				X
▶	02/10	Workin' Away	*	0	0	X
▶	02/09	Spamming Headaches	*	0	0	X
▶	02/08	Comment Spammers	*	0	0	X
▶	02/04	RSS Comes to Teacher Accounts	*	1	0	X
▶	02/03	Problems with Comments	*	0	0	X
▶	01/21	Student Name Security	*	0	0	X
▶	01/17	New Login Procedure	*	0	0	X
▶	01/08	Teacher Bloggers & Education Arts	*	0	0	X
▶	12/22	Featured Articles	*	0	0	X
▶	12/17	What is a Blog	*	0	0	X

e – Comments Manager

Blog Editor Window

Control Panel:

The **Control Panel** tab will display a Control Panel Window that enables you to enter information that will appear on all of your blog pages. You can also upload a class image file, a picture to appear, your and all of your students' blog pages and a personal/professional page that will be viewed only on your pages.

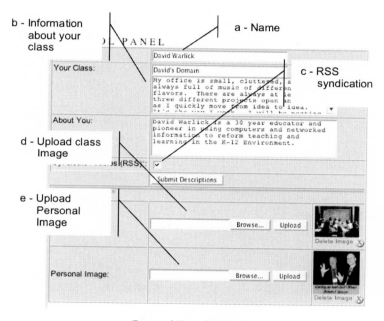

Control Panel Window

The control panel is something that you will set up initially, and then very rarely have a need to return to. This is where you will describe aspects of your site: a description of your classroom (a) (which will appear at the top of all your blog pages), and information about you (to appear in the right panel of your blog pages).

You can also upload a class image (d) for all of your student blogs and a personal image (e) for your blog alone. Just click the corresponding **<Browse>** button and navigate to the image file using the file dialog box that appears. Then click **<Upload>**.

Finally, you have the option of offering RSS syndication. If you click the RSS checkbox on (c), then Blogmeister will build an RSS feed file the next time you add or edit an article and update it each time you edit or add an article. It will also place an RSS chicklet on the front page of your blog.

Class Panel:

The true power of Blogmeister is in the **Class Panel** tab and the Class Panel Window Menu. Here you can add and manage student accounts, read student writings, provide constructive criticism, approve student writings for publication, and fine tune how you want to use the classroom blog site by setting privileges.

MENU

Classes
- Global Settings
- Make Believe Class 1
- Make Believe Class 2
- View Orphans
- Add a New Class

Class Panel Window Menu

The first item on the menu is Global Settings. This is a new feature and at the time of this writing, only one setting is available, **E-mail Notifications**. Some teachers have requested not to receive notifications of student blog postings via e-mail. Unchecking the option stops this feature. To switch it back on, go back into Global Settings and check this feature true.

The next items on the menu are the classes that you have added to your account. To add a new class, skip down to the bottom of the menu and click **<Add a New Class>**. You will be asked for a title for your class. Enter it and click **<Submit>**.

When you click one of your classes, the menu adjusts by adding five additional options.

1. **Basics** – In this form, you can enter a class password for your class. This password will then be required for anyone to be able to read approved blog entries from your students. You can also switch on or off the **List Latest 10 Comments** feature and also RSS syndication for student blogs.

2. **Class Status** – There are two options here for securing student blog articles. Checking the first radio button will make all student blogs available to the public after approved by the teacher. Option two sets all student blogs to require the class password *(set in the Basic page)*.

3. **Comment Security** – This page offers three options for who can post comments on student blogs. The first option requires that the commenter use the class password and teacher approval. The second option requires only the class password, with no teacher approval required *(option two in Class Status must be checked for this to work)*. The third option requires teacher approval for a comment, but no class password.

4. **Display Names** – There are three ways that student names can be displayed. Their entire name (as entered by the teacher), first name and last initial, or first and last initial.

5. **Class Roster** – This page may be considered the heart of Class Blogmeister from the perspective of the teacher. At the top of the window is a form that allows the adding of students to the class. Simply type the student's name *(pseudonym if the student is under 13 years of age)*, a password for the student, and an e-mail address *(optional)*.

Beneath the new student form is a list of the students who have been enrolled in the class. Clicking a student's name will list all of the blog entries submitted or in progress. The center column shows the blog entry's status (published or still editing), and in the right column is a **<Delete>** button, which you can use to permanently delete the blog entry.

If you click a blog title, you will receive a Blog Edit Form. With this form, you can apply minor edits to student blogs and also add comments, which will only

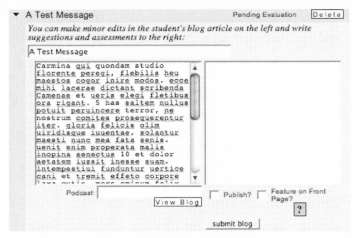

Blog Edit Form

be available to that student. If the blog is ready to be published, then click the **Publish** checkbox. There is also a **Featured Blogs** option on Class Blogmeister. If you check **Feature on Front Page**, that student's blog will be viewable from the front page of Class Blogmeister.

Finally, you can edit student information by clicking the **<Edit>** button by their name. This will produce a Student Edit Form, where you can change the student's name, e-mail address, and student password. You can also elevate a student account to teacher. This feature is only used by staff developers who wish to reset their participants to teacher accounts so that they can add their own classes and students. You can also change the class that your student is registered in, using the drop down that will list all of your classes.

Name: Clovis Muddybluster

E-mail: clovis@someplace.com

Password: br555

New Description:

Account Level: Student

Class: Make Believe Class 1

make change

Student Edit Form

Now if that was too many mouse clicks, do not despair. When one of your students submits an article for publication, you can be automatically informed by an e-mail message. There is a hyperlink embedded in the message that is designed to take you directly into Blogmeister, and directly to the student's article so that you can start assessing their work right away.

In addition, there is a new tab (the next tab) that helps with the regular maintenance of student blogs and comments. Click the **<New Approval Tool>** tab to pop out a new window that will list all pending blog entries or pending comments.

Blog & Comment Approval Tool

Class Students   ⊙ Blog Entries   ○ Comments go

Make Believe Class 1

Clovis Muddybluster
A Test Message
My Day in New York
What I learned today
A New Article
A Test Message for Images

Absence Simpleton

Abby Absentee

Connie Constance
Tuesday's Article

Alvaro Beltran
Confused?

Jamie Jameson

Pending Blog Entries

I have recently started thinking about what might be learned by doing some blind analysis of what the students are doing. One way is to establish tag clouds that display the most frequently used words. The Blogmeister Tag Cloud, below, is a listing of the top 100 words that students have included in their blogs. I initially filtered out words with less meaning, but then decided to leave them in. It might be interesting to see how often students use words like *actually* and *instead*. The words in larger text are used significantly more often than words in smaller text. I suspect that this word map will change as time goes on.

activities actually Alcohol already Amendment america american Another anything article articles available basketball **because** believe blogging BlogMeister century charter children Christopher classroom comment communication computer **computers** content curriculum development different digital Education educational English everyone everything experience favorite Fitzgerald friends generation handheld happened history however important improve information instead instruction internet January knowledge learned learning letters looking members morning nothing outside parents personal playing president probably process professional program project projects published reading remember Research Retrieved Schools Science someone specific started stories student **students** talking teacher **teachers** teaching **technology** thinking thought through together training understand without working writers **writing** written

Blogmeister Tag Cloud

Assessment

This hardly needs to be said to highly trained and practiced educators. So I'll say it only once. Assessment depends on the goals and objectives of the activity. If students have shown mastery of the instructional objectives, then the activity has been a success. Measuring that mastery continues to be a challenge, and this is especially true when the product to be measured is student writing and when the point of the writing is communication.

Weblogs have some features that make them an especially valuable tool for the authentic assessment of student writing. Weblogs are intended for public use, and most include commenting so that real-world readers can provide feedback on the success of the communication. With Blogmeister, even younger children can write to their classmates, protected from the outside world through classroom passwords. Yet the students can easily read each other's writings and respond in a way that illustrates the success of the communication.

As an example, you might assign the class to write a news report on a school, local, or national event – including the five Ws: who, what, when, where, and why. After they have completed their stories, ask the class to read at least two of their classmates' news stories and briefly answer those five questions.

Grading student writing has long been a challenge for busy teachers. It is largely a subjective endeavor with each of us having our own sense of preferred style. Grading rubrics are a wonderful invention to help us evaluate assignments of a more subjective nature.

I will not bore you with an explanation of what a rubric is. If you do not know, then lay this book down and get on the Net. Understanding that students achieve instructional objectives better when they clearly know what those objectives are, it is important that students have access to the evaluative rubrics before they begin their work. There is an easy way to incorporate a rubric into the blog article that you use to make the assignment.

Rubric Machine is another free service of The Landmark Project. This web tool enables teachers to describe the rubric they wish to build and then populate the items with objectives and performance indicators. The final outcome is a grid-style rubric that can be linked to from your blog. But to take things to another level, Rubric Machine also generates HTML code that can be pasted directly into your blog article, causing the rubric to be displayed as part of your article.

Here is how it works:

1. Go to the Landmarks for Schools web site.

   http://landmark-project.com/

2. You will see a blue section to the right labeled *Web Tools*. Click **<Rubric Machine>**.

3. A small web page will appe[...] registered with Rubric Mac[...] name, e-mail address, a pas[...] Then click **<submit>**.

4. Now you can log in by clicking **<login>** and entering your e-mail address and password.

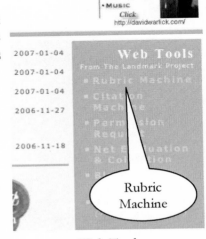

Web Tools

5. You can either make a new rubric or find an existing rubric from the database of assessments created by other educators over the years. If you are giving your students a blogging assignment about China, you might enter China as a *keyword* and click **<submit>**. Twenty-eight rubrics appear, including one called *Rubric for China*. When we select it, we find a rubric with four objectives and four performance indicators by Maritza Suarez.

6. If you want to use this rubric, then you can clone it, as a member, by clicking **<clone this rubric>** at the top of the page. This makes a copy of the rubric that you can edit for your needs.

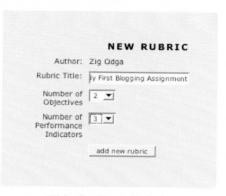

Rubric for China

7. If you want to start a new rubric for your blog assignment, then click <**Make a New Rubric**> from the home page. You will be asked to enter a title for your rubric (descriptive and related to the assignment), and to select the number of objectives you wish to assess and the number of performance indicators for each objective. Objectives and performance indicators can be added and deleted later.

Title for Your Rubric

8. The next page will offer a web form in the shape of a grid-

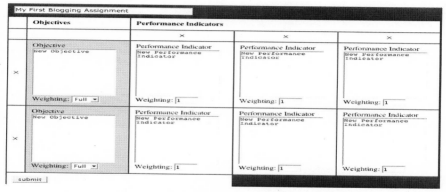

Web form in the shape of a grid-style rubric

style rubric. You can type or paste the objectives and performance indicators here. You can also weight each objective, as some are more important than others, and apply the number of points for each level of performance.

9. After the editing is complete, click **<rubric displays>** at the top of this page. This will list three options for displaying your rubric. They are:

- **Display Rubric as a Web Page** – this will give you a URL that will display your rubric. You can include a link to this URL in your blog assignment so that students can click to it to see how they will be assessed for their work.

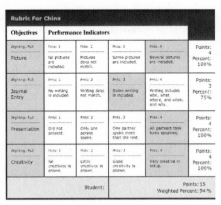

Display Rubric as a Web Page

- **Display Rubric Calculator** – This version of your rubric appears as a form where the teacher or students can select the levels of performance for each objective and then calculate a score based on the number of points and the weighting of each objective.

Display Rubric Calculator

- **Generate HTML Code that will Display** – This display generates and delivers HTML code that will display your rubric directly in your blog article or any other web page on which you can add raw HTML code. For instance, if you are using EduBlogs to write a blogging assignment for your class, you can use this code to include the assessment rubric in with the assignment. Here are steps:

8. Use Rubric Machine to generate the HTML code for your rubric. Highlight the code and copy it into your computer clipboard.

9. As you write your article, EduBlogs is probably set for

Edit Toolbar

10. Place the cursor at the end of this text and paste the HTML code of your rubric there. Then click **<Save and Contiue to Edit>** or **<Save>**.

11. The resulting blog will look like this example of a Rubric-Equipped Blog:

Hello world!

Carmina qui quondam studio florente peregi, flebilis heu maestos cogor inire modos. ecce mihi lacerae dictant scribenda Camenae et ueris elegi fletibus ora rigant. S has saltem nullus potuit peruincere terror, ne nostrum comites prosequerentur iter. gloria felicis olim uiridisque iuuentae, solantur maesti nunc mea fata senis. uenit enim properata malis inopina senectus 10 et dolor aetatem iussit inesse suam. intempestiui funduntur uertice cani et tremit effeto corpore laxa cutis. mors ominum felix, quae se nec dulcibus annis inserit et maestis saepe uocata uenit.

Ceheu, quam surda miseros auertitur aure et flentes oculos claudere saeua negat! dum leuibus male fida bonis fortuna faueret paene caput tristis merserat hora meum; nunc quia fallacem mutauit nubila uultum 20 protrahit ingratas impia uita moras. quid me felicem totiens iactastis, amici? qui cecidit, tabili non erat ille gradu.

Rubric for China				
Objectives	Performance Indicators			
Objective Picture Wighing: Full	Pnts 1 1 No pictures are included.	Pnts 1 2 Pictures does not match.	Pnts 1 3 Some pictures are included.	Pnts 1 4 Several pictures are included.
Objective Journal Entry Wighing: Full	Pnts 1 1 No writing is included.	Pnts 1 2 Writing does not match.	Pnts 1 3 Some writing is included.	Pnts 1 4 Writing includes who, what, where, and when, and why.
Objective Presentation Wighing: Full	Pnts 1 1 Did not present.	Pnts 1 2 Only one person spoke.	Pnts 1 3 One partner spoke more than the rest.	Pnts 1 4 All partners took turns speaking.
Objective Creativity Wighing: Full	Pnts 1 1 No creativity is shown.	Pnts 1 2 Little creativity is shown.	Pnts 1 3 Good creativity is shown.	Pnts 1 4 Very creative in setup.

Rubric-Equipped Blog

Applications

As stated earlier, weblogs are a natural for the classroom, because blogging is about literacy. To blog is to read, think, and write, and then read, think, and write again. When students are blogging as a class, they are writing in order to read, and reading in order to write. It is, in a real sense, a self-sustaining instructional activity of literacy. You just feed in the curriculum by way of the subject matter and engage in the conversation.

> **... weblogs are a natural for the classroom, because blogging is about literacy. To blog is to read and write. When students are blogging as a class, they are writing in order to read, and reading in order to write.**

Here are a few ideas for instructional applications that I have seen in Blogmeister and from other educators who are blogging with their classes.

Portfolio

Because of the "publish, review, comment" structure of weblogs, a classroom blog can make a very effective portfolio. Students submit their writing (and even multimedia), you comment as a way of the assessment, and the work is archived. You might open the portfolio idea up by allowing students to continue to improve their work and request ongoing assessment and constructive coaching.

Student Peer Review

It has long been found by teachers that students are among the most critical reviewers of each other's work, and effectively so. Weblogs are ideal for this type of assignment, where students are asked to write, and then required to read and comment on a specified number of writings by their classmates.

Book Reviews

A media specialist recently told me that she was using weblogs to encourage the students in her school to submit book reviews as blog articles. The rest of the school has access to all of the blogged reviews as an aid in selecting the books they want to read next.

Online Poetry

Quite a few Blogmeister students use their blogs to write original poetry. They will often include scanned original artwork with their articles. Other students and parents are invited in to comment on the students' creativity.

Outside Reviews

Will Richardson, one of the earliest educators to use blogging in his classrooms (and now an author and Web 2.0 Consultant), had his literature students read <u>The Secret Life of Bees</u> by Sue Monk Kidd. Richardson believed that his was one of the first classes to read this book, and thought that the author might be willing to interact with his students. Kidd visited the students' blog articles and then wrote a 2,300-word response for the class discussion. I just did a Google search for this popular title and Richardson's class blog was the fourth hit.[22]

Blogging Artwork

Students can post artwork on their blogs by digitizing them (scanning paper art, or photographing 3D work) and then uploading the image files to ImageShack (http://imageshack.us/). Then the image can be incorporated into most blog tools (including Blogmeister) by typing the following code into the blog, substituting *image URL here* with the URL provided by ImageShack.

<img src="*image url here*" align=right>

Align can be set to *right*, *left*, or *center*.

When the student has blogged the artwork, other students or outside readers can critique the work for the students.

Learning Reflections

Journaling has long been a favorite method by teachers to help students reflect on their continued learning. Asking students to use weblogs for their continued reflections has the added benefit that other students can read and comment on their classmates' ideas. Students might learn from each other's insights.

International Exchanges

Find another class in another part of the country or world and set up a project where students in each site will research and write reports on a national or international story in the news. They will write their blogs as news reports. Then ask the students in the remote sites to comment on each other's reports, looking for evidence that the stories may have been reported differently in their geographic locations. Students could then add additional comments reporting on the differences and try to account for them.

Past Blogs

Ask students to pretend that they are living in the place and time that they are studying in their social studies class, and ask them to write blog articles about events and conditions that they are witnessing. Invite other classes and parents to read and comment on the articles.

Future Blogs

Ask students to pretend that they are living in the year 2100 and they have been asked to identify and describe the "Person of the Century," the person who has made the greatest contribution to the twenty-first century. Students must speculate on what event, invention, or discovery may occur in the next one hundred years that would have the greatest impact on society, then imagine and describe the person who might accomplish it. They should research the skills and education that would logically lead to the accomplishment and include that information in their blog.

Writing Development

When students are writing large reports, essays, or research papers, ask them to submit their rough drafts onto their blogs. Then comment on the papers with constructive criticisms. This is not to say that personal, face-to-face assistance is not needed. The advantage of using a blog is that all comments and developments are archived for study and reference.

Team Blogs

In some cases, it may be more logical to assign teams of students to a blog, rather than individuals. Students could collaborate in creating their articles. Multi-dimensional assignments can be devised that have different team members posting different writings.

Year-End Self-Assessment

As students have spent the year submitting their writings, journaling, and other assignments through their weblogs, ask them at the end of the year to read through their work, and submit a final article, evaluating how their writing has improved over the past nine months.

Podcasting

Podcasting is a popular term for what can most accurately be called *audioblogs*. A podcast, in its most frequent form, is an audio file that can be downloaded and listened to. The person who produces the podcast has usually done so for the same reasons that he or she writes weblogs. It is a way of sharing ideas with a broad or specific audience. Some people use them to return back to their radio days. Others produce podcasts to share original music or the music of their friends. But at its root, podcasting is yet another way that the Internet has become a conversation.

Since the publishing of the first edition of this book, education podcasters have expanded from a handful to countless. On the Education Podcast Network (http://epnweb.org/), an education podcast directory, 165 elementary, middle, and secondary schools have registered their program – and this represents only a mere fraction of the schools and classrooms who are publishing multimedia files to global audiences. Two hundred and five podcasts have been registered by educators who simply want to publish their thoughts and conversations about technology in education and education reform. Once again, this is only a small part of the great multimedia conversation that is happening in the new web.

The first K-12 education podcaster was Steve Dembo (http://teach42.com/), then a technology facilitator in a private school in Chicago. I asked Steve, now the Online Communities Manager at Discovery Educator Network, why he chooses to communicate through his podcast, and in typical Dembo fashion, he wrote a blog about it. Here are some excerpts from that article:

"Why do I podcast when I already have a blog?" I podcast because the spoken word is much more effective for conveying emotion. There are people who share common interests with me (who) are seeking audio content that appeals directly to them; my podcast provides (them) with an alternative to the limited choices available on traditional radio. Most importantly, though, podcasting is a literal voice that complements the virtual voice of my blog.[23]

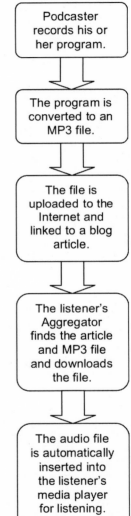

I also produce a podcast called *Connect Learning*. My target audience includes educators. But I also use this audio blog to communicate with parents of students and the general community. I use audio to communicate my message because audio can communicate very effectively, especially since podcast programs can easily be downloaded into personal media players and listened to while taking a walk or driving to and from work.

This brings us to why they are called podcasts. Obviously, Apple's iPod has something to do with it, but there is nothing about podcasting (audio blogging) that requires a Macintosh computer or iPod media player. It is called *podcasting* because the concept arose largely out of the Apple community through a clever usage of RSS syndication. Here is how it works.

The podcast producer records the audio presentation of a message. The producer may also mix in music or other sound resources such as interviews. The recording is converted to a standard MP3

The Podcast Process

file and then uploaded onto the Internet so that it is available for downloading by listeners. A link to the audio file is usually added to a standard weblog, one that offers RSS 2.0 syndication. Version 2.0 carries MP3 links to aggregators in a way that they recognize the presence of an audio (or other media) file.

Originally, special aggregators were developed that could detect MP3 files enclosed within RSS feed files. These aggregators could then be set to automatically download the MP3 file and import it into your computer media player, which can then automatically move a copy of the program into your remote media player.

Shortly after the first edition of this book was published, Apple introduced a version of its iTunes media player application that could do this entire process for you. It even includes a directory of podcasts arranged by subject area. The process works like this:

1. Load iTunes *(Mac & Windows versions are available at http://www.apple.com/itunes/download/)*

2. Click the **<iTunes Store>** and then click **<Podcast>**.

3. The podcast directory will appear, with various topics and a search box. Type *warlick* into the search box to find my podcast, *Connect Learning*.

4. When the podcast appears, a list of the most recent programs will display. Click any of the programs to listen. If you wish to subscribe, then click the **<subscribe>** button by the podcast.

5. Click the **<Podcast>** playlist on iTunes. In the page that appears, you will see *Connect Learning* listed, along with any other podcasts to which you have subscribed.

6. Then the magic begins. As I add new programs to *Connect Learning*, and as the other subscribed-to podcast programs are added, iTunes automatically downloads them to your computer, ready for listening.

7. If you also have an iPod, then the next time you sync your mobile media player with iTunes, all recently downloaded podcast programs will also be copied to your iPod.

It is the automatic nature of podcasting, this marriage between iTunes and individual enthusiasts for almost any topic and publishing their programs about their passions, that has caused the practice to take-off, and to reshape the world of media. Today NPR, BBC, and hundreds of smaller traditional networks are also podcasting their broadcasts to take advantage of our desire to have more control over our media.

Now this is not the only way that podcasting can happen, but it effectively automates the *great conversation*. There are essential two schools of thought on how to use podcasting for teaching and learning. Predominantly at the higher education level, podcasting is being used as a new and adaptive way to deliver content. Many professors are having their lectures recorded and podcasted so that students have continuing access to them after the fact. Some university teachers are recording their lectures prior to the class meeting, and requiring students to listen to them on their own time. Then valuable class time is spent in more interactive endeavors.

One teacher, at a college in New England, invites students to his office after his popular lectures, and they discuss the issues. The teacher records these conversations and then publishes the podcasts as a value-adding endeavor.

In the K-12 world, podcasting is more often used as a way to give voice to what students are learning. Students are asked to further research what they have learned, to write a script, and then record their report. They can then add additional sound effects and even images to enhance the communication, and then publish the program as part of their class or school podcast. One of the most popular and perhaps the very first school podcast is *Radio Willow Web* (http://www.mpsomaha.org/willow/radio/), a podcast from Tony Vincent, of Willowdale Elementary School in Omaha, Nebraska.

Their most recent program, as of this writing, was published on April 25, 2007 (fifteen days ago), and it is an audio report about how our ears work. I didn't know that only animals with backbones have ears.

So how do you make a podcast, post it on the Net, retrieve it, and listen? In the final pages of this book, we will tour a typical podcast, one that I produced last week.

Producing a Podcast Program

The following scenario was based on a true event that occurred about two years ago. I have edited the text from its original version to introduce new podcasting technologies and techniques that have emerged in the last couple of years.

It started on Wednesday, when one of our local TV stations called, wanting to interview someone who was podcasting for a piece they were producing. So Ric Swiner and a cameraman came over, pretty much filling up my small office.

Recording the Podcast

During the interview, while I was demonstrating how I record my programs, the interview gradually shifted to my interviewing Mr. Swiner. To do this, I had an inexpensive USB microphone connected to my computer. I use a Logitech

USB microphone, which costs about $29. I also opened up a program called Audacity. This is a free open source audio editing program that many podcasters use to record and enhance the audio of their podcasts. You can find the program for Windows or Mac at:

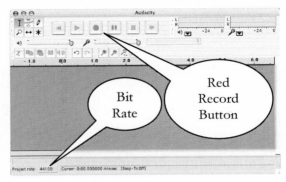

Red Record Button

`http://audacity.sourceforge.net/`

After starting the recording, by clicking the red record button, I asked the reporter why he chose that profession, what he liked about the job, and what makes a good TV journalist. We talked about the art of communication with multimedia. As it turned out, Swiner was also a freelance web developer, giving us even more to talk about.

After the interview was over, I wrote an introduction. I almost always write out the text of my podcasts before speaking them. Personally, I find that I think much better at a keyboard than on my feet. Most podcasters that I know record their programs live with only an outline. If students are podcasting, it might be important to have them write out their reports first, so that you can integrate writing into the activity.

Ric Swiner and I

Here are the steps that I went through to produce that podcast:

1. I connected my Logitech microphone to my computer and opened Audacity. I made sure that the bit-rate was set to 44100, by dropping down the menu at the bottom of the application menu, and then I clicked the red record button to start the recording.

2. As we spoke, a track appeared in the application with the sound waves of the recorded audio streaming across the page.

3. After the recording was completed, I went back and listened to the recording, editing the audio to delete out any unusual pauses or excessive uses of the word "ah!," a big problem for me. You listen to the recording by clicking the purple re-wind button and then the play button.

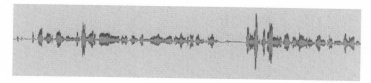

Sound Waves

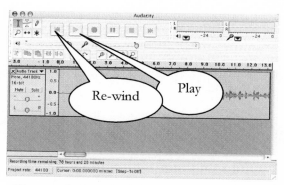

The purple Re-wind and Green Play Buttons

4. Editing the audio is very easy and fun. Simply think of the sine waves as words in a sentence. There is a magnifying glass icon in the tool bar with a plus (+)

symbol in it. Click this button to zoom in on the audio so that you can see individual words and syllables in the audio. To delete a word, highlight it with the cursor (as if you were using a word processor), and press your delete key. Given enough time with this type of editing,

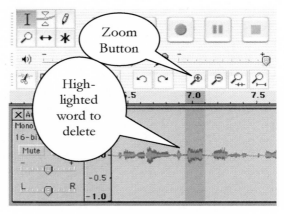

Editing the Audio

I can make myself sound almost intellegent. ;-)

Audacity to edit the audio

5. With a word processor, words can be added, inserted, copied and pasted to enhance the communication. The

same functions are available while using Audacity to edit the audio of your podcast. You can highlight and copy or cut audio from one part of your recording and then paste it to another, by placing the playhead in the position that the copied audio should go *(click the spot to move the playhead)*.

6. To make things even more interesting, you can also add additonal tracks to your podcast that might include music, sound effects, other prerecorded spoken word, or inserted comments. One of my favorite sources of royalty-free sound effects is Partners in Rhyme.

   http://www.partnersinrhyme.com/pir/PIRsfx.shtml

   Here you can download short audio files in categories such as weather, city noises, animals, household and office sounds, industrial sounds, traffic, and transportation.

7. There are many sources for Creative Commons licensed music. The Creative Commons web site includes a page that lists a wide variety of sources for usable music.

   http://wiki.creativecommons.org/Content_Curators

   Other sources include:

   - ccMixter -- http://www.ccmixter.org/

   - PodsafeAudio -- http://www.podsafeaudio.com/

   - Archive.org – http://archive.org

Publishing Your Podcast

In the first edition of this book, this chapter took a great deal of explaining, because publishing your podcast and making your program available to your tens of thousands of listeners was probably the hardest part of the process. There are three essential tasks that you must accomplish to have your program available.

1. A place on the Internet to upload your media (audio or video) files and a procedure (tools and skills) to get your files there.

2. An online presence; a place for people to point their browser to read about your podcast and perhaps click it to listen or watch.

3. An RSS feed that can be subscribed to with a podcast aggregator, such as iTunes. More about this in the next section.

Previously, these were largely three different concerns that had to be addressed separately and with their own set of technologies. Today there are a number of online services that help you achieve all three tasks at one time with one service. I use a podcast hosting service called Slapcast (http://slapcast.com/). It is easy, does everything for me, and the cost is certainly within my budget. At the time of this writing, they charge $4.95 a month with no bandwidth charges, regardless of the number of downloads. They only accept MP3 files and there is a 50Mb file size limit.

The bandwidth issue is important. There are other services that are cheaper or free, but there are limits to the bandwidth, or the amount of programming that can be downloaded by listeners in a single month. There is no problem with bandwidth for most school or classroom podcasts that are being listened to by family and community members. But there is always the possibility that your school podcast will become famous. All it would take is a single amazing program listened to by a blogger with lots of readers listening and writing. Readers then listen and blog, and you suddenly find yourself with 100,000 downloads, and a whopping bandwidth charge or a shutdown of your podcast when your limit has been reached. Chances are slim, but the possibility is there. This is the reason that I pay Slapcast – on the off chance that my podcast could become famous. ;-)

For the sake of this tutorial, I will use podOmatic, that offers free podcast hosting and their operation is relatively simple and straightforward. For free, they provide for 15 Gigabytes of programming download (about 750 downloads of a 20Mb podcast). For $9.99, they provide for 100Gb and $14.99 gets you 200Gb.

We'll go through this process in a straight sequence. First we will set up your podOmatic account, and then upload your first podcast.

Set up podOmatic Account

1. Point your browser to: http://podomatic.com/

2. Click **<Sign-up>** in the top left of the page.

3. You will be asked for your name, e-mail address, gender, date of birth, a username, and a password of at least six characters.

Add a photo, so people know who you are:

Choose a photo:
/Users/davidwarlick/Desktop/images/ Browse...

Upload

Skip for now

podOmatic Image Upload

4. After establishing your account, you will be asked to upload an image for your podcast. This is done in the usual way. You click the **<Browse>** button, find the image using the file dialog box that appears, select it, and then click **<Upload>**.

Adding a Podcast Program to podOmatic

The following steps will be followed each time you want to add a new podcast program.

1. Point your browser to podOmatic (http:/podomatic.com/).

2. Click **<Login>** at the top right of the page to log in to your podOmatic account.

3. Enter your username or e-mail address as the login and your password, and click **<Log In>**.

4. The page that follows offers a button with an invitation to post your first podcast episode. Click this button.

Click for Your First Podcast

5. In the following web form, you will be asked for the following information:

   a. Title: *A representative title for your podcast program. Often Episode 1, 2, 3, etc. will suffice.*

However, you must judge how your listeners will best want to read your titles.

b. Tags: *These are words and phrases that people may use to search to find podcasts on your topic. For instance, if your podcast is about Social Studies, then <u>socialstudies</u> may be a logical tag. Notice that spaces should not be placed in a single tag.*

c. Comments: *Since a podcast is essentially a blog, with an audio file linked in, this will be the body of your blog page. Often this is also called the show notes, and gives you an opportunity to supply links to web resources and explanations that should be posted as text.*

d. Add a Picture: *In some podcasts, you may need to include an image, a photograph, a map, etc. Click the* **\<Browse\>** *button to find the image file to be uploaded.*

e. Show Qualities: *In the checkboxes at the bottom of the page, click to indicate that your podcast is clean. If you click explicit, you will likely attract listeners other than the ones you intend.*

6. Beneath this form is a row of buttons, in gray, that will allow you to upload (import), record (direct through a microphone connected to your computer), or use the mixOmatic. It will even allow you to record video.

a. **Upload:** If you have already recorded your podcast program, click **\<Import\>**. If you have already uploaded the file, then a drop down menu gives you access to that or those files. If you need to upload a file, click the **\<Browse\>** button, then find the file, and **\<Open\>**.

b. **Record:** If you want to record your podcast through your computer, then click **<Record>**. You may receive an Adobe Flash Player warning. Consult your school's technology policies to allow or deny.

Record Tool

After you record the audio, you can listen to it again by pressing **<Preview>** and **<Re-record>** again if it is not to your liking.

You can also click the **<Record Video>** checkbox if you want to record video as well. But I could not get this to work with the video camera built into my MacBook.

c. **mixOmatic:** This is an interesting and useful tool, if you do not have time to mix-in opening and closing music for your podcast, using Audacity or one of the other audio editing programs. Click **<mixOmatic>**, and then select from the music themes (regae, groove, western, rock, anchorman, secret agent), click **<Use it!>**, and then...

7. Finally, click **<Post Podcast>**.

It may take a few minutes for the podcast to actually become published, but when it is, the look of the blog posting is quite impressive. You have a number of templates to choose from, and there is much more here to play around with. Here is a picture of the podcast blog that podOmatic generates.

Episode 1
April 17, 2007 07:49AM

About Me

Frank Warlick

Carmina qui quondam studio florente peregi, flebilis heu maestos cogor inire modos. ecce mihi lacerae dictant scribenda Camenae et ueris elegi fletibus ora rigant. 5 has saltem nullus potuit peruincere terror, ne nostrum comites prosequerentur iter. gloria felicis olim uiridisque iuuentae, solantur maesti nunc mea fata senis. uenit enim properata malis inopina senectus 10 et dolor aetatem iussit inesse suam. intempestiui funduntur uertice cani et tremit effeto corpore laxa cutis. mors ominum felix, quae se nec dulcibus annis inserit et maestis saepe uocata uenit.

Ceheu, quam surda miseros auertitur aure et flentes oculos claudere saeua negat! dum leuibus male fida bonis fortuna faueret paene caput tristis merserat hora meum; nunc quia fallacem mutauit nubila uultum 20 protrahit ingratas impia uita moras. quid me felicem totiens iactastis, amici? qui cecidit, tabili non erat ille gradu.

 Play
Send to Friends | (0) Comments | Download | Permalink

* View profile
* Add as friend

Fans of this show
Become a Fan   View Fans

Contact Info
* podMail: dfwarlick@podomatic.com
* Join my mailing list
* Record a comment

Favorite Links
* podOmatic

Subscribe to this Podcast
* RSS Feed
* RSS 2.0

podOmatic Blog Post

Applications

Here are a number of ways that educators might use podcasting.

Guest Speakers

When guest speakers come to talk to your class, record them, with permission, and produce the recording into a podcast. Then make the podcast available through your classroom web site and through your blog, for parents to access.

Homework assignments

For many, it may actually be easier to speak your daily homework assignments into a microphone, save the MP3 file, and then post it to your classroom web site.

Podcast Lectures

Select content that presents itself especially well as an audio presentation. Record the explanation, and then post it to your blog as a podcast. You may have students who are especially attuned to audio learning. Asking them to record your lectures, to be listened to later, may be useful. If you have lectures that are especially important to the unit and its test, record the lecture along with questions for the class, and post it as a podcast.

Principal's Message

I have heard of a superintendent who started recording a weekly podcast as a way of communicating with the community. He had previously resisted any type of computer-based communication, but podcasting seemed to suit his needs and to suit him. Recently, North Carolina's state superintendent, June Atkinson, has started to publish a podcast of state happenings in education.

Student Podcast Programs

Upper elementary classes might produce a weekly podcast program where they interview each other about what they have learned and what they have accomplished during the week. Middle and high school students might produce a regular podcast out of the media center, talking about media and how it relates to what they are learning.

I believe that this is just the beginning of what this type of push/pull technology might accomplish as the content extends into full multimedia, and the catching devices expand into full multimedia computers. Think about digital textbooks, where content is cast out onto the web through RSS feeds, and students catch the media and organize it in ways that makes sense to them and contributes to the learning of others.

Multi-User Virtual Environments

This is not about blogging or wikis. There is not very much typing involved, nor reading. It has little to do with literacy (at least as we think of it), and the experience is entirely weird for someone of my age. Yet, MUVEs are probably more a part of the emerging technologies conversation today than podcasting was when I wrote the first edition of this book. This month's ISTE *Learning & Leading with Technology Magazine's* cover story is about MUVEs (May 2007).

Question 1: What is a MUVE?

There are a number of acronyms that represent pretty much the same thing: MUD (Multi-User Domain), MOO (Multi-User Object Oriented), MUSE (Multi-User Simulated Environment), and, my favorite, MUSH (Multi-User Simulated Hallucination). MUVE is probably seen most often in our conversations because we can easily substitute *Environment* with *Education – Multi-User Virtual Education.*

The concept has been around for many years, since before the World Wide Web, when people where entering, building, and competing inside of text-based virtual realities. You logged into the MUD server, and were instantly confronted by the description of a place, which you had to read.

> You are standing in a wood-paneled room. Before you is a wooden desk with a drawer. On top of the desk is a leather-covered book. To your right is a door to a patio, and to the left is a locked door.

From here you could type, "go right" to pass through the door to the right and into the patio, where you would confront a new description. You might also type, "read book," where upon the description of your room would be replaced by text from the book.

You might also type, "open drawer." Text would appear such as,

> You have opened the desk drawer which, though resistant, finally yielded to your persistent tugging. Inside the drawer you find a brass key.

If you type, "get key," you can now go through the locked door to the left. If another player entered your wood-paneled room, a line of text would be added to the room description announcing that, "Chaulla is standing in the corner behind you." You could then type a quotation mark and then a message, and Chaulla would read, "Pei (my online name) says, 'Hello, Chaulla. How did you find yourself here?'" If you type a colon and, "jumps up and down with joy," Chaulla would read, "Pei jumps up and down with joy." So the environment becomes not just an adventure, but also a social network.

A handful of education researchers at MIT and in Arizona tested these text-based environments with promising results, as students were challenged to create their own virtual environments by describing them. The richness of your environment depended on the richness of your descriptions.

Alas, the web came along and then Mosaic and Netscape, and surfing the web became the *chose préférée à faire du jour*. Over the years, a number of attempts were made to revive the genre, especially projects to create graphical user environments, most notably, Activeworlds (http://activeworlds.com/).

The technology advanced on top of an emerging genre of video game called MMORPGs (Massively Multiplayer Online Role Playing Games), where children (and young adults) played in their game environments online, with teams or guilds of other players, playing from around the world.

The MUVE that is currently attracting the most attention is Second Life, produced and managed by a small software company in San Francisco, Linden Labs. I currently enjoy an office on EduislandII, somewhere in this ever-expanding virtual universe, along with, at this writing, 6,240,591 other residents. 34,219 residents are logged on at this writing, at 2:19 in the afternoon, EST.

One of my online friends is entirely blue. Another one looks like a very short otter with very long toenails. I tried to capture, to the best of my ability, my own look. I'm Suriawang Dapto.

Suriwang Dapto

One of the interesting aspects of Second Life is their business plan. They sell virtual real estate. You pay for it with Lindens, their currency, which you can buy with U.S. Dollars, and probably other real world currencies. My office is part of a building paid for by Kevin Jarrett, a researcher studying the educational value of MUVEs with a grant from Walden University.

Question 2: What does this have to do with the New Web?

The simple answer is that MUVEs are not part of the new web, because they are not on the web. They are special server/client applications that operate parallel to the World Wide Web. Still, MUVEs are about collaboration and content. It isn't words and pictures that residents are building, but a place where people can meet, invent, explore, entertain, teach and learn. It is about conversations, about user constructed and controlled content, and people find each other here because of their ideas. I've made several friends in the past few days, among them educators from Denmark and Slovenia.

Question 3: Can teaching and learning take place here?

This is a most important question. My answer is, "yes!" But will children be sitting at their desks building and conversing in virtual environments during the school day? Probably not. But in much the same way that children were developing their writing skills by building text-based virtual domains in the early MUDs, children could probably learn special problem-solving and programming skills in Second Life, all within the context of building assignments about novels read, historic events studied, and scientific concepts discovered.

In Second Life, I am currently using my office as a waypoint for visitors who have attended my workshops and presentations. There is a typewriter that I built, by digitally fashioning seven primary shapes into a 1910 Royal typewriter. If you click the typewriter, it is programmed to launch your browser and load my blog. There is also an antique Slovenian radio on my table, which, when clicked, will load and play my latest podcast.

I have just finished a file cabinet with a file drawer for each of my most often requested workshops and presentations. When clicked, the drawer will slide open, your browser will be launched with the online handouts for that presentation, and then the drawer will close.

The mathematics involved in changing the positions of the drawer to give the illusion of a working file drawer, were fairly dense but basic. It occurs to me that students might build objects that can slide or roll around on the floor of an office or an outdoor field. These objects could be programmed to interact with each other, in such a way that students are starting to use mathematics to create virtual robots, perhaps even robotic soccer players. How else might math students be motivated to do that much math, challenging each other to learn?

A Final Word

This emerging information environment seems to be impacting us in ways that few could have imagined only a handful of years ago. Because of the degree to which we have come to depend on digital information, and our growing influence over the information environment, it has become critical that we include in our instruction the ethics of how we access, use, and communicate information.

So I want to leave you with a final tip. Spend some time talking to your students about the good and the harm that can be done with information, and then ask them to pledge that they will only use information to help people. On the next page is a sample pledge that you might ask them to read and sign.

Blogger's Contract

Acknowledging that blogging is a legitimate and authentic form of journalistic publication, student and teacher bloggers must adhere to essential principles of ethics. The free exchange and publication of information can help people in important ways. At the same time, information can also harm people either intentionally or unintentionally.

Being a responsible participant in **the great online conversation**, I pledge that I will use information to:

❑ Honestly and joyously express the truth, and that if challenged, I will be able to prove that what I write or say is true,

❑ Always treat all people with respect. I will never use information to cause harm or appear to cause harm to any person or group of people, and

❑ Respect and protect information tools and that I will neither do any harm to a computer system, network, software, or other person's information; nor will I allow others to do harm to a computer system, network, software, or other person's information.

❑ I will always be accountable for the information that I produce and publish, willing and able to defend my information or acknowledge when I have made a mistake and fix it.

_____   _____

Teacher   Student

We are about the **conversation**. As people (consumers, citizens, teachers, learners, each of us dealing with daily affairs) we are all ultimately responsible and we should be a part of the great conversation – Kindergarten through retirement.

I hope to hear from you!

Appendix

Blogging & RSS Resources

Blogging Tools

Blogger, Blog*Spot	Web-based	Free
LiveJournal	Web-based	Free $25/y premium
Radio UserLand/Manila	Software	$39.95/y
TypePad	Web-based	$4.95/m Basic $8.95-$14.95 Premium
Movable Type	Install on your server	$150 Free for individuals & Nonprofits
WordPress	Install on your server	Free

RSS Aggregators

NetNewsWire	Software Mac	$39.95
SharpReader	Software Windows	Free
Staw	Software Linux	Free
Bloglines	Web-based	Free
Newsgator	Web-based or Software	Online is Free

Podcast Aggregators

iPodder1.0	Software Windows Mac	Free
iPodderX	Software Mac	$19.95 Free version
Doppler	Software Windows	Free
Pod2Go	Software Mac	$12.00

Notable Education Bloggers

I tried on several occasions to compile a list of the top education bloggers, but there was no way around personal bias. So I am deferring to another list, one compiled by Dr. Scott McLeod, Director of the Center for the Advanced Study of Technology Leadership in Education (CASTLE), and author of Dangerously Irrelevant. In January of 2007, McLeod analyzed data from Technorati that includes the number of blogs that link to edubloggers, producing a ranked list. In reality, this is a dynamic listing, but for the sake of this resources, I am putting it on paper.[24]

Inside Higher Ed – http://insidehighered.com/
Weblogg-ed – http://insidehighered.com/
Stephen Downes – http://www.downes.ca
2¢ Worth – http://2cents.davidwarlick.com
Cool Cat Teacher – http://coolcatteacher.blogspot.com
Moving at the Speed of Creativity – http://www.speedofcreativity.org
Tuttle SVC – http://www.tuttlesvc.org
Purse Lip Square Jaw – http://www.purselipsquarejaw.org
Elearningspace – http://elearningspace.blogspot.com
Learning Now – http://www.pbs.org/teachers/learning.now/
Eduwonk – http://www.eduwonk.com
EduBlog Insights – http://anne2.teachesme.com
Think:lab – http://thinklab.typepad.com/think_lab/
Bgblogging – http://mt.middlebury.edu/middblogs/ganley/bgblogging/
Around the Corner – http://www.edsupport.cc/mguhlin/blog/
The Fischbowl – thefischbowl.blogspot.com/
A Difference – http://adifference.blogspot.com/
Christopher D. Sessums – http://elgg.net/csessums/weblog/
Education/Technology – http://tim.lauer.name/
Remote Access – http://remoteaccess.typepad.com/
Dangerously Irrelevant – http://scottmcleod.typepad.com/
The Learning Circuits Blog – http://www.learningcircuits.org/
Teach42 – http://teach42.com/
Practical Theory – http://www.practicaltheory.org/serendipity/
The Quick and the Ed – http://www.quickanded.com/
TechLearning Blog – http://www.techlearning.com/blog/
Infinite Thinking Machine – http://www.infinitethinking.org/

Too many are missing, so here is what's in my aggregator:

Joyce Valenza – http://joycevalenza.edublogs.org
EdCompBlog – http://edcompblog.blogspot.com/
Edu.Blogs.Com – http://edu.blogs.com/edublogs/
EdTechUK – http://fraser.typepad.com/edtechuk/

ICT in Education – http://www.terry-freedman.org.uk/
Teaching Hacks – http://www.teachinghacks.com/
Strength of Weak Ties – http://jakespeak.blogspot.com/
Cog Dog Blog – http://cogdogblog.com/
Connectivism – http://connectivism.ca/
Sega Tech – http://segatech.us/
Sharon Peters – http://www.mtl-peters.net/blog/

Index

X

Y

Works & Resources Cited

1 Drury, Tom. "Blogs over Baghdad, or: Where is Pax Salam ?." St. Petersburg Times ONLINE 30 Mar 2003. 25 Mar 2005 <http://www.sptimes.com/2003/03/30/Perspective/Blogs_over_Baghdad__o.shtml>

2 Maass, Peter. "Salam Pax Is Real." SLATE. 2 Jun 2003. 25 Mar 2005 <http://SLATE.msn.com/id/2083847/>.

3 Rosen, Jay. "The Legend of Trent Lott and the Weblogs." PRESSthink 15 Mar 2004. 25 Mar 2005 <http://journalism.nyu.edu/pubzone/weblogs/pressthink/>.

4 "People of the Year: Bloggers." ABCNews 30 Dec 2005. 27 Mar 2005 <http://abcnews.go.com/WNT/PersonOfWeek/story?id=372266>.

5 Sifry, Dave. "The State of the Live Web, April 2007." [Weblog Sifry's Alerts] 5 Apr 2007. Technorati. 1 Jun 2007 <http://www.sifry.com/alerts/archives/000493.html>.

6 Horrigan, John. "Home Broadband Adoption 2006." PEW Internet & American Life Project. 28 May 2006. PEW Charitable Trusts. 7 May 2007 <http://www.pewinternet.org/PPF/r/184/report_display.asp>.

7 Zuiker, Anton. "Blogs - A Short History." Blogging 101 - An Introduction to Reading & Writing a Weblog. 27 Feb. 2004. University of North CArolina. 27 Mar. 2005 <http://www.unc.edu/~zuiker/blogging101/>.

8 Blood, Rebecca. "Weblogs: A History & Perspective." Rebecca's Pocket. 7 Sep. 2000. 27 Mar. 2005 <http://www.rebeccablood.net/essays/weblog_history.html>.

9 Quintas, Peter, and Peter Kaminski."True Voice." Non-Profits Blogging. ITConversation, . 25 Mar 2005. Audio Archive. 27 Mar 2005 <http://www.itconversations.com/shows/detail439.html>.

10 Allard, J. "The Future of Games: Unlocking the Opportunity." 2005 Game Developers Conference. Moscone West Convention Center, San Francisco. 9 Mar 2005.

11 Anderson, Chris. [Weblog The Long Tail] 1 Jul 2007 <http://www.thelongtail.com/>.

12 Sifry, Dave. "State of the Blogsophere, August 2006." Sifry Alerts. Argent Hotel, San Francisco. 7 Aug 2006. Technorati. 18 Sep 2006. <http://www.sifry.com/.../archive/000436.html>.

13 Warlick, David. "When do I Blog?." Exactly 2¢ Worth. 21 Mar. 2005. The Landmark Project. 13 Apr. 2005 <http://davidwarlick.com/blog/index.php?itemid=188>.

14 Bloglines. Google. 13 Apr. 2005 <http://bloglines.com>.

[15]Horrigan, John. "Home Broadband Adoption 2006." Pew Internet in American Life Project. 28 May 2006. PEW Foundation. 21 Apr 2007 <http://www.pewinternet.org/PPF/r/184/report_display.asp>.

[16] Horrigan, John B. "Trends in Internet Adoption and Use: Comparing Minority Groups." OTX Research. 11 May 2004.

[17] "Jimmy Wales." Wikipedia. 13 Dec 2006 (last edit). Wikimedia Foundation. 13 Dec 2006 <http://en.wikipedia.org/wiki/Jimbo_wales>.

[18] Giles, Jim. "Internet Encyclopaedias go Head to Head." News@Nature.com 14 Dec 2005 20 Dec 2006 <http://www.nature.com/news/2005/051212/full/438900a.html>.

[19] Carvin, Andy. "Turning *Wikipedia* into an Asset for Schools." [Weblog Andy Carvin's Waste of Bandwidth] 11 July 2005. 22 Dec 2006 <http://www.andycarvin.com/archives/2005/07/turning_wikiped.html>.

[20] McKenna, Brendan. "High School Bans Blogging." Rutland Herald 29 Mar 2005. 18 Apr 2005 <http://www.rutlandherald.com/apps/pbcs.dll/article?AID=/20050329/NEWS/50329 0316/1027>

[21] "Rubric Builder." Rubric Builder. The Landmark Project. 14 Apr. 2005 <http://landmark-project.com/rubric_builder/>.

[22] LiCalzi O'Connell, Pamela. "Can Johnny Blog?." The New York Times 14 Aug 2003 8 May 2007 <http://www.nytimes.com/2003/08/14/technology/circuits/14diar.html?ex=13761936 00&en=eaa8f00c728408a0&ei=5007&partner=USERLAND>.

[23] Dembo, Steve. "Why Podcast When You Already have a Blog?." teach42. 5 Apr. 2005. 12 Apr. 2005 <http://www.teach42.com/2005/04/05/why-podcast-when-you-already-have-a-blog/>.

[24] McLeod, Scott. "Top Edublogs?." [Weblog Dangerously Irrelevant] 29 Jan 2007. 1 Jul 2007 <http://www.dangerouslyirrelevant.org/2007/01/top_edublogs.html>.